HUMAN RIGHTS IN INDIA

HUMAN RIGHTS IN INDIA

Discourses and Contestations

Edited by

K. S. PAVITHRAN

GYAN

First Publication in 2018

Published by

Gyan Publishing House
5, Ansari Road
Daryaganj, New Delhi-110002
Phone: 9811692060
E-mail: books@gyanbooks.com

Printed at: G. Print Process, Delhi.

Cataloging in Publication Data—DK
Courtesy: D.K. Agencies (P) Ltd. <docinfo@dkagencies.com>

Facets for Human Rights in India (Seminar) (2017 : Calicut, India)
Human rights in India / by K.S. Pavithran.
pages cm
Papers presented at a seminar conducted by the Department of Political Science, University of Calicut, Kerala on Facets of Human Rights in India on January 31 and February 01, 2017.
Includes bibliographical references.
ISBN: 9788121214346 (HB)

1. Human rights—India—Congresses. I. Pavithran, K. S., editor. II. University of Calicut. Department of Political Science, organizer. III. Title.

LCC KNS2095.F33 2017 | DDC 342.54085 23

Contents

Preface and Acknowledgements

The concept of Human Rights is an ancient creation but it became central to the political debate in the modern age. Discussions on human rights are attracting both intellectual discourse and discussions among activists and politicians. Human Rights are commonly understood as inalieanable, fundamental rights to which a person is inherently entitled simply because she or he is a human being. The struggle to preserve, protect and promote basic human rights continues in every generation in every society. In this sense human rights are rooted in the history, culture and values of every nation. However, human rights and related issues got universal acceptance after the proclamaiton of Universal Declaration of Human Rights by United Nations in 1948. Since the adoption of the UN Universal Declaration of Human Rights, states have been committed to advancing human rights. Seven different UN treaties, signed by majority of world's states are also in existence for the advancement of human rights in the world. But the fact is that brazen disregard for the importance of human rights is the prevailing reality in different parts of the world. This was mainly because, as Maurice Cranston in his celeberated essay 'Are there any human rights?'[1] points out that human rights need to have a restricted reference to only the 'first generaton rights'. To him the traditional political and civil rights are not difficult to institutionalise for the most part, they require governments and other people generally to leave a men alone — The problem posed by claims to economic and social rights however, are of another order altogether.

India being a diverse country with its multiculture, multi-ethnic and multi-religious traditions developed a universal perspective of human rights. Gandhi who led the Indian freedom movement made non-violance (Ahimsa) an integrated part of his life and work. B.R. Ambedkar was a champion of human rights by upholding the rights of the 'low castes'. India is a signatory to majority of human rights agreements and pacts and has been playing a major role in the United Nations in protecting and promoting human rights. Indian Constitution promises to secure the rights of all sections and strive for liberty, equality and fraternity. However, India is still witness to caste, class, gender, cultural and regional disparties. The fact is that, sizeable segments of its population are socially marginalised and remain excluded from basic human rights. The societal structuring based on *Varnashrama Dharma* excludes large segments of population and consequently members of the 'low castes' victims of social exclusion and resultant human rights violations. Further, the three decades of development experience based on neo-liberal economic policies has thrown up several challenges to the development debate itself.

Development initially aimed at rapid growth with a dose of distributive justice developed into a system abetting with capital. Globalisation in fact more than becoming 'panacea' has accentuated the disparity as well as differences among people. It is estimated that in India around 2.5 lakh farmers has committed suicide between 1990s and 2000s. The Special Economic Zones, have dislocated millions of people including Tribals, Dalits and farmers from their land. Priviatisation of natural resources including water is another threat. Instead of a provider, the State became a facilitator for global capital, thus colluding with corporates in the midst of series of human rights violations.Consequently, the tribals have been progressively losing their rights to their lands, homes, forests, traditional source of livelihood, cultural practices etc. The conditions of women, children and minorities are not better now. Addressing these challenges are important in the present context. People especially the marginalised, the Dalits and Aadivasis began to protest vehementally against human rights violations both from corporates and from state itself. To handle these conflicts, the state is always depending on force instead of solving the issue through peaceful negotiations and welfare measures. The repressive measures included arbitrary laws, more powers to the police and para-military forces. These conflicts have resulted in a spurt in people's movements in the country. This has led to large number of civil society groups, including the new social movements, contesting disputing the claims of globalisation and neo-liberal economic policies and the subsequent arguments about, or of expanding the Human Rights.

Thus the plight of human rights in India is marked by 'normalisation of exception'. The growing war and terror for protecting national security and public order brought forward a number of Acts like the Terrorist and Disruptive Activities (Prevention) (TADA) Act, The Prevention of Terrorist

Activities (POTA) Act and Armed Forces (Special Powers) (AFSPA) Act., it is argued in violating the civil and political rights of the citizens of India, as well as the activists struggling on behalf of the citizens as part of vibrant human rights movement in India. In short, nowadays, the growth of market based economy with neo-liberal agenda have posed newer challenges to the idea of human rights. Large number of people have become the victims of the new development paradigm initiated by the globalisation and global capitalism. In these circumstances, the democratic institutions should be used appropriately to ensure that there is an equal stake for all the citizens in the process of participatory governance to minimise the human rights violations.

The present volume is the result of a seminar conducted by the Department of Political Science, University of Calicut, Kerala on 'Facets of Human Rights in India'. The Essays in this volume covers different aspects and issues related to human rights in India which include theoretical discussions on human rights, Human rights issues related to development, environment, climate change, water, social media and cyber world.

In preparing this volume, I have incurred too many debts to acknowledge here. Foremost, I would like to thank all the contributing authors for a great learning process. I owe great debt to Prof. Valerian Rodrigues for sharing his scholarship and expertise in the seminar on 'Facets of Human Rights in India'. I do thank all my friends for their active co-operation and generous support, especially to Dr. J. Prabhash, former Professor and Head, Department of Political Science, University of Kerala and Dr. Ajit Dayanandan, Professor, University of Alaska Anchorage, United States. I wish to express my deep gratitude to the students at the Department of Political Science, University of Calicut who attended my classes in 'Marxian Political Theory' and 'Indian Political Process' and the discussions on human rights issues. Thanks are also due to my colleagues Jisina T.K and Anjali Devi. M. A word for Sreejith. K for his patience in typing the manuscripts of all my works. Finally I am obliged to Gyan Publishing House, New Delhi for undertaking the responsibility of bringing out this edited volume.

K.S. Pavithran

List of Contributors

Prof. P.L. Dharma, is Chairperson, Department of Studies in Political Science, Mangalore University, Karnataka. His areas of Specialization and Research are Political Sociology, Identity Politics, and Public Administration. He has been Visiting Professor at the K.M. Centre for West Asian Studies and Indian Ocean Studies, University of Calicut, Kerala (2010-12) and Director of Gandhian Studies Centre, Mangalore University (2005-2012). He is also the Director of Budhist Study Centre of the University from 2005 onwards.

Prof. Valerian Rodrigues is currently Ambedkar Chair at the Ambedkar University Delhi. He is known for his seminal work on Babasaheb Ambedkar (The Essential Writings of B.R. Ambedkar, Oxford University Press, 2010) and for his formulations of themes in Modern Indian Political Thought. Rodrigues has made substantial contributions to the debate on the working of the Indian Parliament (with Sankar B.L.,The Indian Parliament: A Democracy at Work, Oxford University Press, 2014) and constitutionalism in India, and agrarian politics in India. He received his PhD from the Centre for Political Studies, JNU, in 1986, and was Agatha Harrison Fellow at St. Anthony's College, Oxford from 1989-1991. He was also a senior fellow at the Indian Institute of Advanced Studies, Shimla, from 1999-2001. Rodrigues taught Political Science at Mangalore University, Karnataka from 1982 to 2003 before moving to Jawaharlal Nehru University, New Delhi. As a Professor (2003-2015) at the Centre for Political Studies at JNU, he was popular for his lectures on Indian and South Asian Political Thought, and critically reading the same through political concepts of modernity, secularism and nationalism. He is also National Fellow of the Indian Council for Social Science Research (ICSSR). He has been the ICCR (Indian Council of Cultural Relations) Visiting Professor at the University of Erfurt, Visiting Professor at the University of Wurzburg and Fellow at the Max Weber Center for Advanced Studies, Erfurt, Germany.

Prof. John S Moolakkattu is Head of the Department of International Relations and Dean, School of Global Studies, Central University of Kerala. He was earlier Director of the School of Gandhian Thought and Development Studies, Mahatma Gandhi University, Professor at IIT Madras and Gandhi-Luthuli Chair Professor in Peace Studies at University of KwaZulu-Natal, Durban, South Africa. He has been Commonwealth Scholar at Bradford University, UK and Commonwealth Fellow at Lancaster University, UK. He is also the editor of Gandhi Marg, the Quarterly Journal of the Gandhi Peace Foundation, New Delhi.

Prof. K.S. Pavithran is currently Professor and Head, Department of Political Science, School of Social Sciences, University of Calicut. He has also Director of K.M. Centre for West Asian Studies and Indian Ocean Studies, University of Calicut. Spanning an official career of over 36 years, he has published three books— *The Janata Interludes (1990), Non-Aligned Movement: Unipolar World and Beyond (2007), Foreign Policy and Martime Security of India (2013),* and contributed several articles in reputed journals and edited volumes. His areas of research include Marxian Political Theory, Indian Political Process, Secularism and India's Foreign Policy. Dr. Pavithran is the General Editor of the ISDA Journal: Studies in Development and Administration and Editorial Board Member of *Puthuvazhi* the quarterly Journal of Pratheeksha Trust, Member Editorial Advisory Board, International Journal of Political Science and South Asian Journal of Socio Political Studies. He has served as a Member of the Governing Council of the Kerala State Higher Education Council during 2008-2012.

Prof. Sudha Mohan is currently Professor and Head, Department of Civics and Politics, Mumbai University. Her areas of Interest and study are Comparative Politics, New Politics of Identity, Urban Politics in the age of Globalisation and Development Discourse. She has been BPC Fellow at Centro de Estudos e Pesquisas BRICS-BRICS Policy Centre, In Rio de Jeneiro, Brazil in 2013, Visiting Scholar under the framework of Research Excellence Program, USC, India (PEIN) at the University of Santiago de Compostela, Spain in 2013, Visiting Faculty in the University of Osnabruck, Germany from 2011 to 2013., Visiting Faculty in the School of Humanities and Social Science, University of St. Gallen, Switzerland in 2014. She has also awarded the Nirman Visiting Fellowship at University of Westminister, London, awarded the Sr. Fullbright Fellowship by the United States Department of State's Bureau of Education and Cultural Affairs and the Foreign Fullbright Scholarshp Board in Washington, DC (2004-2005)

Ms. Nirmala V U is pursuing Ph D in Center for Political Studies, Jawaharlal Nehru University New Delhi. She was formerly associated with Department of Political Science, University of Calicut as Lecturer in Political Science. Her areas of research interest include Religion and Politics, Environmentalism, and Left Politics.

Dr. Anju Lis Kurian is UGC Post Doctoral Fellow, School of International Relations and Politics, M.G University, Kerala, India. She has published several articles in international and national journals. She was awarded The National Young Political Scientist Award 2015 by the Indian Political Science Association. She is the editor of the mRNA-a multidisciplinary journal.

Dr. C. Vinodan is currently Honorary Director, Institute for Contempoary Chinese Studies (ICCS) at the School of International Relations and Politics, Mahatma Gandhi University, Kottayam. He is also serving as Chairman, Centre for Strategic and Security Studies (CSSS) SIRP and Coordinator, Rajiv Gandhi Chair for Public Policy Studies. Dr. Vinodan was a Post-doctoral Research Fellow at the Department of Political Science, University of Kerala during 2001-2003. Dr. Vinodan was a Visiting scholar (Fulbright Project) at the Claremont Graduate University, California (USA) in 2003. He won the Fulbright American Studies Institute (FASI) Fellowship during 2000 at the University of Delaware, Philadelphia. Vinodan was also the recipient of the Regional Centre for Strategic Studies (Colombo) Summer Award in 2000 and had secured the Ford Foundation Teacher Research Grant in 1998.Dr. Vinodan is the Project Director in a Major Research project (2010-11) on "Nuclear Deterrence and National Security in South Asia: A Study on India's National Security Strategy" by the Indian Council for Social Science Research (ICSSR), New Delhi. He is also the Principal Investigator in a UGC sponsored Major Research project on "Energy Security for the Emerging India: A Study on the Problem and Prospects on expanding the nuclear option." Dr. Vinodan has contributed several articles in national and international journals/books etc and attended many conferences/seminars/workshops held in India and abroad.

Dr. Devi Parvathy working as an Assistant Professor in Department of Public Administration and Public Policy, School of Social Sciences, Central University of Kerala. She has served as Project Fellow on the UGC-SAP project titled Globalisation, Ethnicity and Religious Fundamentalism in South India, Department of Political Science, University of Kerala. She has Published several articles in National and International Journals and contributed a Chapter in the edited book titled Globalisation, Stateand Governance. Her Area of Specialisation are Governance, Public Policy, Development Administrationand Human Rights.

Ms. Anjali Devi M is a research scholar in the Centre for South Asian Studies, Jawaharlal Nehru University, New Delhi. Her interest areas include non-traditional security challenges, climate change and sustainable environment. Her publications include "Climate change in India: A non-traditional security perspective" in the Journal of Polity and Society and she has also contributed a chapter titled "Climate Change as a non-traditional security threat: A case study of Pakistan" to the edited volume of "Climate Change on Developing countries" published by Cambridge Publishing House. She is also associated with the Department of Political Science, University of Calicut, as a Guest Faculty.

Dr. Sabu Thomas is working as Assistant Professor in Political Science, Government Brennen College Thalasseri and a research supervisor at University of Kannur. He was a post-Doctoral Fellow at Centre for Political Institutions Governance and Development, Institute for Social and Economic Change Bangalore. His area of interest include ICT& Society, Human Rights& South Asian Politics. He has published a number of articles in journals and periodicals and as book chapters. He has also presented papers in National and International conferences. He was a guest speaker at the International Workshop on Social Policy and Social Protection in Asia 2015 at Hong-Kong Institute of Education, Hong Kong, July 27, 2015.

Dr. Ashalekshmi B.S is Assistant Professor at the Department of Public Administation and Public Policy, School of Social Sciences, Central University of Kerala. She got Ph.D from the University of Kerala in Public Administration.Though her area of research is E-Governance, she specializes in the emerging areas of Governance and Gender Studies. She has been an Assistant Professor in Jain University, Bangalore. She presented papers in many national and international seminars and has a good number of publications in the areas of e-governance, good governance, gender issues, higher education and sustainable development Apart from academics, she had experience in the media also as anchor and director of Women Empowerment programmes.

Dr. Shaji Varkey is Associate Professor at the Department of Political Science, University of Kerala, Thiruvananthapuram. He was the Director of V.K. Krishna Menon Centre for International Relations, University of Kerala during 2009-2012. He was also visiting scholar at Claremont Graduate University, USA in 2007. He has several international collaboratory projects to his credit. Presently, he is working on a project on Spaces of Political Protests in Kerala, sponsored by Indian Council of Social Science Research (ICSSR), New Delhi. His major publications are in the field of international relations, development and environment.

1

Human Rights Experiments in India: An Introduction

— *P.L. Dharma*

Introduction

The package of Human Rights as conceived and implemented by the United Nations has successfully reached to designated places though it was not seriously considered at the execution level. The idea, conceptualization and implementation of Human Rights at global level is widely appreciated and encouraged and considered from all corners to be one of the political priorities over the years. It is also regarded as the major breakthrough in the history of human kind to protect and preserve the existence of human beings. The experiments on Human Rights elsewhere suggested the fact that there is an incomparable liking for Democracy. Both Democracy and Human Rights can easily travel hand in hand. However, the intervention of United Nations in making it what it is today is a remarkable exercise of this century. Human Rights experiments are not per se are mere experiments of Rights. There is a history, politics, culture, public acts and a mixed response within it. The United Nations being the premiere world body representing the voice of every living being has been a major force of influence on the nations across especially in implementing the Human Rights agenda. This demonstrates the relevance as well as the power of United Nations on one hand and on the other the obligations of member nations towards United Nations across the world. Given its vivid roles played for all these years, the UN has the distinction of being highly normative, humane and concerned for voiceless across the world. Human Rights is one of its agenda through which United Nations has been demonstrating the role of a Critique, Rebel, and an Eye opener of several nations. Its role in levelling criticisms against individual nations with regard to the poor management of Human Rights is seen as the unquestionable Courage to monitor the performance of individual nations with regard to Human Rights.

Obligated to this tradition of United Nations being very critique of poor players of the world, many countries learnt to be working with in the broad frame work of Human Rights. India is one of the political realities of the world paid a humane respect and considered Human Rights as one of its major political agenda and priorities. The democratic agenda of India received a boost with Human Rights journey. Being a signatory to the cause of Human Rights India not only institutionalized the effort to define and protect Human Rights but also committed to keep it lively through several state agencies. Both National Human Rights Commission(NHRC) and State Human Right's Commissions (SHRCs) reflected the institutional pattern of Human Rights on one hand and on the other joined hands with the global effort of adding meaning to it. The commissions both at the centre and states ensured that they function with the reasonably defined autonomy to do justice to their existence in India. The list of issues and cases handled by respective commissions hitherto defined the nature and scope of Human Rights in India.

Indian experiments

In an ideal situation HRs act as a binding force where each and every one irrespective of what she or he is brought under one umbrella. The spirit of oneness as human beings is widely appreciated. It acted as a binding force, a bridge to work against the gaps between people and more than that it brought a new political culture of oneness. Given India's socio economic and colonial experiments making way for HRs though was a risky and impossible task, India accepted the package and began to adopt it in its unique democratic political setup. Without making a significant changes in its principle and concern India attached an institutional shape to the HRs package. Thanks to the expertise by the legal luminaries of India who guided and conceptualized how the package has to travel in India. Accordingly, the HRs was welcomed with the strong institutional structures and expected to functions as per the established rules and regulations. The functional pattern of NHRC and SHRC attracted the attention of people from all walks of life in their initial stage. Thanks to the role of civil societies of different nature who took up the issues of HRs more seriously than the official institutional patterns. Civil society intervention in the HRs discourse broadened its scope as well as problematized the issue more seriously than ever before in India.

While the institutional structures of HRs began to educate younger generation on HRs through academic exercises the civil societies highlighted the major issues concerned with HRs. One among them is the gross violation of HRs which was considered to be part and parcel of Indian society. It further highlighted the excess caused by the state and its different agencies at different levels and assessed the damage on HRs.. While state and its agencies engaged in their act of infringing in to the rights of individuals and justified the same, the civil societies termed it as the state sponsored violations. There are clear instances to substantiate this and to prove a fact that the HRs debate and activities in India is basically a skirmish between the state and civil society.

However, the character of the Indian society especially the Caste and economic character have posed a major challenge to the HRs journey. Instead of uniting people as the one the socio-economic realities treated every one not only as a separate individual but also as either superior to one or inferior. The inherent hierarchy constructed and practiced in Indian society could not tolerate the provisions created for the HRs and its mission against the inequality in India. As a result, the class which involved since ages in ill treatment of people on the equation of caste and class began to look at the HRs agenda as anti-hence, attempted to promote alternative forces against the HRs. Indeed, the state was seen as the promoter of the special provisions which protected the unprotected and was attacked tooth and nail. Besides, the dominant class worked to propose all possible alternatives to the state which stood like the representative of poor and exploited. Attack on the state was thus attack on the agenda of the state. On the other hand as contradictory, the state was criticised for and regarded as he greatest enemy of Human Rights in India. This double edged attack on the HRs package continued as the contradiction and effected its implementation. The attack on the state both as the protector of unprotected and the violator of HRs is an unending contradiction. Due to this the HRs debate is called the debate on private and public debate. The private is represented with the strong sense of anti-state feeling as the state is accommodating the social diversity with social dignity. The public on the other hand is a weak force which defends the state in an era where the neo liberal forces have much say.

Besides, Indian society has had few cases which was qualified as the violation of HRs. There are a few cases or instances of violations which was recorded or reported. The nature and numbers of the reported cases at the level of commissions are not very little and they suggest the fact that the rate may increase. Some of the examples of the cases reported are custodial deaths, excess on Adivasis during the state initiated search operations and evacuations, caste abuses and the delay in justice. The commissions have initiated actions and spread the message of strict and legal actions on those indulged in coming in the way of HRs. The inbuilt social practices if viewed from the angle of HRs have enough to demonstrate the fact that violations are socially rooted and have become the social practice. The hidden violations and the violations exposed and recorded are different both in nature and implications. The poor and the unprotected have climbed the ladder of social change by making use of the programs of the state. The presence of the poor and unprotected in places which was occupied by the upper class and socially dominant groups generated a situation where the exploitation was revised and innovative methods were used. Thus, abusive languages replaced the physical torture in the process of exploitation of unprotected. The institutional pattern of HRs did not have the space for handling the verbal attack by the dominant over the dominated.

The state in India thus, has further ensured the justice to all irrespective of social categories. Some of its policies are testimonial to the same. However, state has been in receiving end and had to take the blame as the key source of HRs violations. State has been taken for tasks when state violates and simultaneously justifies the violation especially when it begins its expansion project. As it is often highlighted, the state justifies its excess in the name of law and order to keep the larger community safe and secured. The state has become the centre, the centre of controversies. Its actions are taken for debate from different perspectives and often hardly allowed to implement its projects.

One of the major agencies of state often taken for task is the law and order department. Both the police and defence forces deployed to manage the crises ridden areas have often stepped out and used force, intimidated and in few cases abducted. The violent behaviour of the law and order forces is the major highlights of the HRs debate in India today.

Any attempt either from a public or a private institution where it has the tone of working against the life and living mode of any one is seen as the greater threat to HRs elsewhere. In India, it has been reduced to the debate between private and public sphere especially between the state and non-state actors. At least the experiences reveal that HRs violations are witnessed every time when state designs and implements its development agenda.

On the other hand, the civil society began to watch every step initiated by the state and evaluated hitherto the way state behaved to prove its authority over its citizens. According to the civil society the culprit is state in India. It is this state that has caused the greatest damage to the Rights. Thus, the state is the supreme violator of Human Rights. State is also called as the instrument of exploitation in India.

Though the non state agencies have heavily came down on the acts of state, they believed in the fact that the presence of the state is essential. The state, to all non state actors is the primary enemy of HRs for it violates its own creations as well as those which are naturally bestowed on individuals. If the state is the culprit why the state has did what it did for years. Though to certain extent state played the role as both making [?] and breaking of what is qualified as HRs the state has justified its intentions.

State in India is not only a larger political reality but also a system of conglomeration of the social reality. The social plurality within the state is the naked reflections of the Indian society. Thus, an element of attacking the state is also attacking the social reality. State as the guardian of the constitution does not entertain any force comes in its way of extending benefits to people of all sections.

The defence of the state and the charges levelled against the state by the non state actors are to be stressed to get in to the crux of the problems of HRs debate in India. The following are the areas proposed to raise the debate in HRs experiments.

1. Is Indian state full of rules and regulations to be qualified as the welfare stare
2. Is Indian state a representative of the Indian society?
3. Are non states actors are drawn from different ideological and political backgrounds?
4. Are non states actors are exhibiting the intolerance?

Conclusion

The moment India became the signatory to the HR it is understood that India accepted the rules and regulations that constitute the HRs. In this context, the violation means violation of the established rules and regulations which promises the good life to all the human beings. The trust is violated, the spirit is violated, the idea is violated and the philosophy is violated. The state may violate, individuals may violate and any agency may involve in an act which violate the existing rules and regulations. The following are the reasons why in India HRs are easily violated-

1. There is inherent inequality in society
2. The caste is the major source of violence
3. Economic inequality has supported caste to escalate violence
4. The democratic practices did not find roots in social contexts
5. The existing inequality is treated as the natural
6. India celebrates the inequality as part of the cultural practices
7. Inequality is treated as ones own fate
8. Inequality is a matter of pride as it deals with history, and finally
9. HRs violation takes place as it is not taken seriously by the culprits.

These issues need to be tackled not from the broad fame work of HRs but in the context of Indian society.

2

Modes of Oppression and the Expanding Regime of Human Rights in India

—*Valerian Rodrigues*

Human Rights are a specific variant of rights. They stipulate that all persons in a society are entitled to certain claims as human beings, and conversely, one cannot be fully human if denied these claims. They might include significant economic and social freedoms such as those enumerated in the UN charters or in the Indian constitution back home. In this context it is important to draw attention to several economic and social rights expressed in Directive Principles of State Policy which the court has pronounced as fundamental rights over time such as, for instance, the right to education and the right to livelihood. When claims are accepted as rights others have a binding obligation to respect them, superseding other interests (In the playful words of Ronald Dworkin, 'rights are trumps', ensuring victory, *ab initio*, to their claimant). The state is obliged to frame laws and mechanisms for the enforcement of these rights.

While human rights call on us to defer to certain claims, those who make such claims may assign different significances to them. These differences are asserted because while humans want to be fully so, what it means to be fully human may widely vary. Therefore while freedom of choice of employment is a basic human right for a liberal, Gandhi would argue that pursuing one's occupation handed over to him is essential for swaraj. A basic human right of choosing an occupation will be read differently by Gandhi and a liberal protagonist. Therefore, difference in perspective on what constitutes human ends can reorder the regime of human rights differently. Where there are differences in perspectives with regard to prioritisation and significance of rights, it is important to involving the concerned parties in determining the shared domain of rights, and the extent to which they would like to remain different. Such involvement cannot be merely consultative but participatory. In this regard, one of the most vexed issues in India is uniform civil code. Often uniform civil code is pitted against the right to be different, i.e., choose ways of life, markedly at variance from those of others. In fact deeply different societies such as India have no alternative but to constantly engage in democratic deliberation to mark off the arena of uniformity, and the arena where people would choose to be different.

All social objectives cannot be regarded as human rights. According to Amartya Sen, the social objective claimed as a human right must be of sufficient importance to form the constitutional norm of a society as a standard of achievement, the realization of which would provide legitimacy to the behavior of all agents and authorities, especially the state. The objective should also be 'coherent' so that the obligations or duties that have to be carried out, and the agents who have to do so, can both be specified. Human rights trump other social objectives. The obligations that human rights impose are binding and if an agent does not carry them out he is susceptible to reprimand and sanctions. If these obligations are incorporated in the domestic legal system then this mechanism would be legal and settled in a court. If the rights are recognized in international human rights law then states as parties are bound by it.[1]

Human rights cannot be seen merely through the juridical mode. If they are not adequately institutionalized then to work towards them may form part of the obligation generated by the recognition of these rights. Such obligation is founded on good reason which people tend to accept with fairness in view. "Human rights generate reasons for action for agents who are in a position to help in the promoting or safeguarding of the underlying freedoms."[2] A person can be held morally accountable if he or she derelicts his/her duty arising from human rights.

It might be pertinent to say, that in our context, where the world has increasingly closed upon itself, human rights remain the only moral codes that can keep people otherwise divided, across nation-states, religions, ethnicities and classes, together. While there could be disagreements with regard to human rights, both its content, relations and significances, there could still be agreement on certain basics, and issues of departures.

A. Expansive Nature of Human Rights

Globally the sphere of human rights has hugely expanded over the last century. India as a party to a vast body of these rights, conventions, treaties, declarations and agreements also defers to this body of rights, although many of them may not be positivised in terms of domestic law. This is the case for instance with regard to rights of internally displaced persons. Many of these rights involve vulnerable sections such as women, Dalits, Adivasis etc. India has also accepted provisions and regulatory frames proposed by many UN bodies such as on physically challenged persons. In fact much of the legal provisions that India has enacted on physically challenged persons are follow on to international agreements in this regard.[3]

In the domestic political arena there has been a systematic attempt to replace the welfare language with rights discourse. The watershed moment in this regard was 1990s and early 2000s. After independence India's political discourse was dominated by the distinction between civil/fundamental rights on one hand and social welfare on the other. The Congress Party had perfected this distinction in embracing scores of populist measures, and sometimes pitting it against the great constitutional institutions in India, such as the Supreme Court. Often association was made between civil and fundamental rights with private property and capitalism and populism with socialism. The shift to rights language was very evident when the Indian State attempted to arm itself with more and more draconian laws against terrorism,[4] and against the complicity of the state agencies in communal riots in Gujarat. Speaking against Prevention of Terrorism bill in the joint sitting of the house, Sonia Gandhi (Cong- L.S) argued that the Bill under discussion was meant, "to project the issue of national security as a tool, as a partisan tool of propaganda" and it clearly "violated basic human rights."[5] Its use as a partisan tool was demonstrated particularly in Gujarat following the Godhra killings and subsequent communal carnage. She said, "To begin with, POTO was used to ban organisations in a partisan manner...The Gujarat Chief Minister used it in a astonishingly sectarian manner, namely, against only those perpetrators of the killings of Godhra. He did so on the basis of contrived distinction that one set of victims were the victims of terrorism and the other set of victims were actually the victims of rioting."[6] A volley of legislation came to be passed in 2000s employing the rights language, particularly Mahatma Gandhi National Rural Employment Guarantee Act (MANREGA), Panchayat Extension to Scheduled Areas (PESA) Act, The Scheduled Tribes and Other Forest Dwellers (Recognition of Forest Rights) Act, Land Acquisition, Resettlement and Rehabilitation (LARR) Act etc.[7]

While the shift of language from welfare to rights was facilitated by a set of complex developments in 1980s and 1990s[8], The Supreme Courts language had registered a shift towards the rights-language in the post-emergency period, after the tragic complicity of the Court in sustaining an authoritarian regime in judgements such as *ADM Jabalpur*. In the *Maneka Gandhi* case the court upheld the principle of 'due process of law' when Justice Bhagwati pronounced that the procedure established by law in Article 21 must satisfy the test of being 'just, fair and reasonable' as expressed in Art. 14. Subsequently, the court has closely guarded the domain of rights as its sphere of authority. In the *Vishaka Case* the Supreme Court confronted with the persistent problem of sexual harassment at the workplace issued several directions and *virtually enacted a law* on sexual harassment. In *Waman Rao v Union of India* the Court declared that laws passed for giving effect to Directive Principles under Article 39(b) and (c),dealing with social and economic equality, did not weaken the basic structure but strengthened it. It thereby placed the conflict between the Parliament and judiciary, if any, not on the issue of equality and liberties but on other grounds. This stand of the Judiciary was to eventually become the mainstay of the Court's wisdom in subsequent years. With regard to minority rights while there is much prevarication by the Court, it has generally taken a position that these are a special class of rights and enjoy a degree of precedence, although they have to respect certain stipulations such as common citizenship and rule of law.

The 1990s and 2000s have also seen setting up a large number of bodies explicitly based upon invocation of human rights, such as the National Human Rights Commission, the National Commission for Women, the Minority Commission, the National Commission on Children, the Central Information Commission etc. There was also the splitting up of the SC&ST commission into two bodies. A large number of states too in India have set up parallel bodies for the purpose. Looking at the functioning of these bodies one can only say that these agencies could be much more imaginative than they are at present.

A large number of non-governmental, voluntary organisations emerged particularly from late 1970s onwards, many of them ostensibly committed to the defence of human rights. Certain relatively marginal groups such as Dalits, Adivasis, and Muslims too threw up organisations in defence of rights. Organisations such as All India Muslim Personal Board, and Dalit Solidarity network, National Alliance of People's Movements have been important interventions in this regard. Recently the Home Ministry has announced that India has about 3.4 million registered NGOs, a number that probably exceeds the number of schools that India has. Such an expansion of the sphere of human rights in India should have made them the national commonsense. However, this is far from the case. Why? To answer this question we may have to take recourse to a concept, oppression.

Modes of oppression and actual shrinking of the space of human rights

Iris MarionYoung employs the concept of oppression to denote the overlapping structures that stand in the way of human rights. She identifies five such categories: "exploitation, marginalisation powerlessness, cultural imperialism and violence". Exploitation denotes the the mode of surplus appropriation from direct producers through prevalent production relations. Through marginalisation "a whole category of people is expelled from useful participation in social life and thus potentially subjected to severe material deprivation and even extermination". A large number of them such as the old and the infirm come to be dependent on government bureaucracies for support and services. Powerlessness denotes the inability of people to decide their course of life. They rarely participate in decisions that directly bear on their lives. Such a condition offers little possibility of developing one's capacities or revalue one's course of life: "The powerless have little or no work autonomy, exercise little creativity or judgements in their work, have no technical expertise or authority, express themselves awkwardly especially in public and bureaucratic settings and do not command respect." Through "cultural imperialism the dominant meanings of a society render the particular perspectives of one's group invisible at the same time as they stereotype one's group and mark it out as the other". Those who are subjected to cultural imperialism are defined from outside, while at the same time they are cast as the interiorized others. For some groups fear of being subject to violence is their everyday life experience. They live under fear of "random, unprovoked attacks on their persons and property which have no motive but to damage, humiliate, or destroy the person". They are also subject to subtle forms of harassment, intimidation and ridicule.[9] In India we can cite many social groups living in the condition of such subjection and marginality, such as internally displaced persons on account of majoritarian violence and living in refugee camps, people thrown out of their hearth and home on account of caste violence, or the bonded labour as a social category.

Given these modes of oppression, the agents themselves who are caught up in these structures find extremely difficult to claim their rights. It makes the expansion of rights merely formal. Only those who can muster enough resources against the structures of their oppression succeed in securing their rights, and those who can muster such resources are few. But these few are not homogenously distributed across diverse modes of oppression. Modes of oppression and the subjection and marginality they beget throw up their own distinct hierarchy built around levels of segmentation. But since there is a small stratum that finds access to right-claims in every group they in turn rope in the entire group into one or the other rung of the hierarchy. Indian democracy, unlike the political society of Partha Chatterjee, still embodies the principle of graded inequality.[10]

The diversity of India, particularly religious, linguistic and cultural, informs such a regime of rights its characteristic specificities. We generally hear in Muslim parlance that formally Muslim women are better endowed with rights by Koran, Hadith and the Sunnah compared to their counterparts in other communities. Unfortunately, a large number of Muslim women in India are governed by local customs rather than Sharia laws. Those who interpret these laws and issue fatwas are generally men. Muslim women have little capacity to make their own right to ijtehad heard, and heard loudly. And although laws like the Muslim Personal Law (Shariat) Application Act, 1937 and other laws are supposed to grant Muslim women rights and protect them from discriminatory customary laws, the absence of codification of Muslim personal laws has resulted in many of the rights granted in religious texts getting suverted or diluted. Creating conducive conditions in a context of oppression requires an enabling setting that Amartya Sen captures in the concept of capability.

The bureaücracy in India is little attuned to make room for expansive rights. Traditionally Indian bureaucracy is not merely beholden to power but also to dominant interests in society. It is wetted by democracy and rule of law far too little. If we look at the processes of demonization of vulnerable groups by the bureaucracy, it becomes clear.

Increasingly the civil arena in India is captured by groups who have little regard for rights. They have their interests to serve which may find expression in loud claims of nationalism, ethnicity and identity. The violence that oozes out of such expressions can often make a mockery of any claim of rights. A specific public culture that is invasive is effortlessly taking hold of our sensibilities and dispositions. Such invasiveness could be on account of technology, or the compelling force of images and representations that tend to direct our course of affairs rather than we deciding the course of events. The former seem to have made our choice already and we believe it is our choice. This is particularly the case where means of communication and dissemination enjoy a monopoly.

In a world of unimaginable flow of information and outreach what we confront is the ghettoisation of the human: This involves drawing up barricades around ethnicity, language, religion, nationality, gender etc. This process has often gone hand in hand garnering prejudices and 'othering'. Demonization of minorities across many societies today is just one of its expressions. In the Global arena we live in times when human rights regimes assiduously built over the years are finding doors shut against them by new-found assertions of nationalisms, religious belonging or ethnicities. The concept of human autonomy is under seize.

There are also perceptible signs of a philosophical turn that denies human persons a centrality. The significance of persons now lies only in being part of structures and processes. In this context we may have to make a distinction between two modes of constitution of persons: The first ascribes a self-hood to persons anterior to sociality; the second sees it as constitutive of the social relations in which one is placed. Claims and dispositions of human self vary depending where one lays one's stress on. But both these stances need not deny human rights.

Making Human Rights Agenda Viable

In a thin sense human rights are truly universal: All humans form a single species, have certain basic needs, sentiments and emotions, in common. Under appropriate conditions all humans have displayed capacities of reasoning and choosing the purposes of their own life. While moral disposition of people may widely vary, generally all unprejudiced observers tend to agree what is a valuable life to live and what not. It is still in cultural domains expressed in political communities that human rights find their cultural embeddedness. Human rights therefore need to speak to culturally embedded societies. In this context societies need to discover their own traditions of human rights. One of the powerful such journey was the one inaugurated by Raja Rammohan Roy. But one could very well argue, that eventually the idea of freedom or gender equality central to Roy's imagination was limited. There could be alternative traditions of anti-caste movements that one can tap, or something of the *Aklaq* tradition that Sir Syed Ahmed Khan posited. There are also the powerful folk traditions that offer us platforms of egalitarianism. Such attempts will not necessarily convert human rights into an ethnographic agenda, but may hold forth an ideal of what human being could be.

Notes and References

1. See Amartya Sen, "Elements of a Theory of Human Rights", *Philosophy and Public Affairs*, Fall (2004), Vol. 32, No. 4, pp. 315-56.
2. *Ibid,* p. 319.
3. There is provision of 3 per cent reservation to physically challenged persons, and the Supreme Court had to wield its whip repeatedly on this issue. There are poor estimates of the extent of physically challenged persons in India, which may even exceed 8 percent of India's population. Often the approach to these people is not through the lens of rights, but patronization. There is widely prevalent social customs in India of refusing to admit the fact of physical deformities, and even hiding these people from social interactions. Increasingly, a significant proportion of these physical disabilities are engendered in India by exposure to or consuming substances that are vulnerable, such as for instance pesticides, or exposure to nuclear minerals in the Jharkhand-Orissa region.
4. *Joint Sitting of the Houses of Parliament*, Vol. 1, March 26, 2002, Lok Sabha Secretariat, New Delhi. POTO was a law proposed in succession to a series of harsh laws curbing citizenship rights in India, such as Maintenance of Internal Security Act (MISA) in 1970s and TADA, enacted in 1985. TADA was extended from time to time and in 1995 it was allowed to lapse.
5. *Ibid.,* pp. 29-30
6. *Ibid.,* p. 29
7. Incidentally, there was an attempt to describe India as a liberal democracy during this period. The relation between rights language and market freedoms are problematic. While liberal democracy need not necessarily be associated with market freedoms, this was largely the case in the political discourse in India.
8. Globalisation, the decline of socialism, a shift to deontological approach to considerations of justice and rights etc.
9. Iris Marion Young, *Justice and the Politics of Difference*, Princeton, Princeton University Press, 1990, pp. 39-65.
10. For Partha Chatterjee's conception of Political Society, see, *Wages of Freedom*, New Delhi, Oxford University Press, 1998, pp. 9-17 and *The Politics of the Governed*, Ranikhet, Permanent Black, 2006, pp. 27-41.

3

Gandhian Approach to Human Rights

— John S Moolakkattu

Gandhi is seen by most people as a champion of Human Rights and has been a source of inspiration for movements for freedom and rights in many parts of the world, notable among them being the civil rights campaign in the US led by Martin Luther King Jr. Gandhi commenced his political life with the conception of the citizen as a bearer of rights and privileges. When he was thrown off the train at Pietermaritzburg for insisting, as a coolie, to enter a first-class cabin for which he had purchased a ticket, realisation came to him that, as an Indian, he had no rights in South Africa. For the rest of his life, Gandhi would remain deeply committed to a political struggle to secure equal rights for all Indians, first within the British Empire and then as free subjects of an independent India. At the commencement of his political career, as Gandhi strove to secure rights for Indians in South Africa, he also undertook to inquire into the duties that might correspond with the rights claimed by those who were the victims of injustice. "During the first year," wrote Gandhi in *Satyagraha in South Africa*, "I was merely the witness and the victim of these wrongs. I then awoke to a sense of my duty". He rejected the exclusive association of citizenship with the demand for rights. Gandhi's thinking was not embedded in the human rights discourse of the Western liberal world within which the modern notion of rights has been framed.

Judith Brown writes:

> Gandhi came from a very different philosophical background. The tradition of Hindu political thinking was highly developed and sophisticated. But it had no rights discourse and did not place major

emphasis on the value of the individual and his or her protection and development. Its concerns were far more with communities than individuals (2006:.238).

Every right is accompanied by a corresponding duty to ensure that the right is acknowledged, respected and protected. In recent years, in the field of international law, there is a growing realisation to remind nations of their duties to citizens, on the non-performance of which, clauses like responsibility to protect are invoked.

In this chapter, I shall venture to make an analysis of Gandhi's perspective on human rights. Rights theory is known for its focus on protection of individual freedom vis a vis the state. Logically, it was deeply skeptical about society and the humanity at large. Protection against the forces coming from the state and society that constrain an individual's full development is the goal of human rights.

In 1940, Gandhi asked HG wells, who had sent him a charter of rights of man for his suggestions, to "Begin with a charter of Duties of Man ... and I must promise you that rights will follow as spring follows winter" . He later said writing in Harijan, 'If all insist on rights and no duties, there will be utter confusion and chaos". He also added that rights that do not flow from duty are not worth having. At the same time, Gandhi always accorded special attention to individuals, which he claimed was his supreme consideration, and often had personally attended to minute details of others including children.

Gandhi received a western legal education and held great admiration for such western thinkers as Tolstoy, Ruskin, and Thoreau. Gandhi's thinking was not founded upon western liberal human rights discourses centered on the freedoms of individuals, but upon Indian philosophical traditions that was aimed at protecting the community as a whole. The above thinkers who influenced him were early critics of the liberal order. Gandhi's worldview emphasized dharma—as performance of our duties to the people around us—as a way we can achieve true swaraj. According to Gandhi, people have no natural individual rights, only rights earned through the performance of duty, as he understood all individual humans to be interdependent.

The appropriation of Gandhi for human rights causes, according to Judith Brown, is based on a simplified picture of Gandhi's thought (and his life). She thinks that Gandhi had altogether different goals for humanity than human rights proponents. "For them rights are the device for protecting core values and attributes of individual and group life, vis—vis the forces of the state and society. For him recognition of individual duty and social and moral interdependence were the foundation of an authentic human existence" (Brown, 2006). In Gandhi's worldview human rights must first be earned by performing duties. For the majority of the world's peoples "Human Rights" in the western sense were unattainable until the method in which the wealthy minority lived changed.

Porat says:

> Rights-talk and duty-talk are no doubt expressions of much wider worldviews regarding political temperament and the essence of humanity. The language of rights expresses liberal values such as self-realization, liberty, individual autonomy, free competition and maybe even an ounce of hyper-individualism and egocentricity. A person becomes a human being by virtue of pursuing and claiming his due. By contrast, the language of duty emphasizes the crucial importance of self-restraint, the aspiration to virtue and solidarity. A person is a human being by virtue of fulfillment of the responsibilities he bears (2015: 8).

Nineteenth-century liberal and Italian patriot Giuseppe Mazzini, one of the most famous men of his age, titled his central volume of moral and political theory *The Duties of Man* (1860), which Gandhi adds as suggested reading at the end of Hind Swaraj. Mazzini wrote in the book :

> I merely say that such rights can only exist as a consequence of duties fulfilled, and that we must begin with the latter in order to achieve the former....Hence, when you hear those who preach the necessity of a social transformation declare that they can accomplish it by invoking only your rights, be grateful to them for their good intentions, but distrustful of the outcome(Quoted in Moyn, 2016).

Now to emphasize too much on duty and the community as opposed to individuals is seen as paving the way for fascism and authoritarianism. This is not what Gandhi wanted. Instead he wanted to create an enabling order of freedom, which came not from a direct assertion of rights, but based on the performance of certain duties including the duty to resist. The concept of duty is equally applicable to the oppressor and the oppressed. The oppressor has the duty to stop the oppression, and for the victim the duty to resist it. By presenting rights in terms of mutual obligations that all human beings have towards one another in a state of interconnectedness, Gandhi presented an alternative approach to the question of human rights. In this scheme, the apparent right to resist an unjust ruler would cease to be a right, but a duty to protect people and uphold the moral order (Brown, 2006).

It is also pertinent here to say that Gandhi did not consider group rights to be important. If that were the case, he would have taken a more lenient view in the matter of separate electorate for dalits in 1932. For him such a right is also an assertion of breakage with the interconnectedness.

Liberation in Gandhian view is not just liberation of the individual from social constraints- but also liberation of oneself. Gandhi's rural India sought to privilege the traditional occupations carried out by the Harijans that involved manual labour. Its implications for the dalit cause has not been properly understood. In sum, Gandhi's approach to questions of human rights and social justice were founded upon an associative approach built on the foundations of a relational world view as opposed to the modernist dissociative strategy of Dr. Ambedkar. Ambedkar's approach had focused on rights as claim-making in the liberal sense and did not seem to have any faith in stirring the obligations of the caste Hindus towards the oppressed. Stirring the responsibility of the oppressors to repent and make amends for the wrongs committed is an integral part of Gandhian emancipatory agenda.

It is not surprising that libertarian theorists such as Robert Nozick (1974) provide little scope for obligations to society. But the lack of attention to social duty is somewhat puzzling in theorists who propose more egalitarian principles of distribution. For example, John Rawls says that he is concerned with identifying the principles that assign "rights and duties in the basic institutions of society" and that define "the appropriate distribution of the benefits and burdens of social co-operation" (Rawls, 1971: 76). But he does not say much about duties and even less about the distribution of the burdens (as opposed to the benefits) of social cooperation. The same neglect is found in Ronald Dworkin and Bruce Ackerman. Thus the language of 'duty' has almost entirely disappeared from stabdard political vocabulary. Indeed, in a world where identity politics thrives on its insistence of rights for distinct political, ethnic, racial, linguistic, or religious groups, the very notion of duties has been rendered obsolete.

Parel (2006) says that Gandhi held that modern notion of rights and duties should be presented in relational rather than oppositional terms. In making duties first like means, Gandhi departs from liberalism which lays stress on individual rights. In liberalism, rights are based on a reciprocity principle among self-interested individuals rather than based on relationality, that is, if we are going to make a claim, we also have to admit that an equal claim belongs to everyone else failing which it will be seen as a privilege.

If Gandhi held on to the position that rights flow from duties, he was not blind to the obvious circumstance that compelled historically deprived groups to perform duties without having any rights conferred on them. The burden of exercising duties falls most heavily on those who occupy the most privileged positions in society, and accordingly Gandhi could admit the possibility that those who have been deprived of rights should have fewer duties devolved upon them.

In 1947, Gandhi was asked to state his views on human rights for the UNESCO compendium on the subject. He wrote: "I learned from my illiterate but wise mother that all rights to be deserved and preserved came from duty well done" (Cited in Roberts, 2015: 141). Gandhi added. "In swaraj based on ahimsa, people need not know their rights, but it is necessary for them to know their duties. There is no duty but creates a corresponding right, and those are true rights which flow from a due performance of one's duties" (CWMG 75:178).

The Bhagavad Gita had exercised a tremendous influence on Gandhi's life and he studied and interpreted the text carefully. The Gita, one could say, is a set of teachings, delivered by Krishna to Arjuna on the eve of the great battle around which the Mahabharata epic has been woven together, about the performance of one's duties, without attachment and without any heed to the rewards that might follow.

Gandhi considered freedom as synonymous with self-rule and he integrated into his notion of freedom the notion of obligation to others as well as to oneself insisting also that voluntariness should be the very basis of freedom. Self-rule thus implies the voluntary internalization of our obligation to others which will be impossible if we are imprisoned by our selfish desires(Iyer, 1983).

In Vivekananda also freedom and social responsibility are seen as intimately linked so as to bring in harmony. Each person's quest for liberation must entail service to society, what Gandhi would later call the idea of Sarvodaya or upliftment of all. Aurobindo said: "It was a marked feature of the Indian mind that it sought to attach a spiritual meaning and a religious sanction to all, even to the most external, social, political circumstances of its life, imposing on all classes and functions an ideal, not except incidentally of rights and powers, but of duties, a dharma with a spiritual significance" (1966: 7-8.).

Gandhi drafted for the Congress in 1931 an extensive "Resolution on Fundamental Rights" that constituted the most explicit defense of civil liberties. Gandhi's position is that civil rights and liberties must be grounded in a prior sense of civic duty. If not, they may either remain dormant among an ignorant and apathetic population or assume a dangerous attitude in a democracy. Western rights theorists, beginning with Locke, have affirmed that freedom is not "a liberty for every one to do what he lists, to live as he pleases, and not be tied by any laws," but it is freedom under law and the source of civic obligation is founded in law. (Locke,1980, p. 17). Gandhi accepts this position, that in an independent India obedience comes from" voluntary acceptance of the rule of law in the making of which the whole of India had its hand through its elected representatives"(CWMG 89:112). Gandhi valued highly the role of law when derived from popular sovereignty. Yet his concept of swaraj demanded a form of social and political responsibility that Locke never required, a commitment that was much closer to Rousseau: the obligation to change oneself and one's community for the betterment of all, in a spirit of social service.

Gandhi uses this theory of dharma to shape his idea of rights: "Having a right surely does not mean that I should exercise that right in utter disregard of my sense of proportion... The exercise of right depends on one's sense of duty. It is my duty to follow dharma... I do what I consider my duty" (CWMG 69:208). This is a sequel to what he had said in Hind Swaraj that "real rights are a result of performance of duty" and that in England everybody was "insisting on his rights, nobody thinking of his duty" (CWMG 10:44). He said that Hind Swaraj was written "to offer a glimpse of dharma," to persuade India and the world at large to order life to in such a way as to develop a sense of moral obligation. After his assumption of the leadership of the Indian national movement, he wrote : "One's respective dharma towards one's self, family, nation and the world cannot be divided into watertight compartments. The harm done to oneself of one's family cannot bring about the good of the nation. Similarly one cannot benefit the nation by acting against the world at large... Therefore it all starts from self-purification. When the heart is pure, from moment to moment one's duty becomes apparent effortlessly" (CWMG 50:370).

At a prayer meeting in Delhi, Gandhi referred to the work of the Constituent Assembly and remarked: "The Constituent Assembly is discussing the rights of the citizen. That is to say they are deliberating on what the fundamental rights should be. As a matter of fact the proper question is not what the right of a citizen are, but rather what constitutes the duties of a citizen. Fundamental rights can only be those rights the exercise of which is not only in the interest of the citizen but that of the whole world. Today everyone wants to know what his rights are, but if a man learns to discharge his duties right from childhood and studies the sacred books of his faith he automatically exercises his rights too. I learnt my duties on my mother's lap. She was an unlettered village woman...She knew my dharma. Thus if from my childhood we learn what our dharma is and try to follow it our rights look after themselves... The beauty of it is that the very performance of a duty secures us our right. Rights cannot be divorced from duties. This is how satyagraha was born, for I was always striving to decide what my duty was" (CWMG 88:230).

In a subsequent meeting Gandhi said: "Yesterday, I talked to you about duty. However, I was not able to say all that I had intended to say. Whenever a person goes anywhere certain duties come to devolve on him. The man who neglects his duty and cares only to safeguard his rights does not know that rights that do not spring from duties done cannot be safeguarded. This applies to Hindu-Muslim relations. Whether it is the Hindus living in a place or Muslims or both, they will come to acquire rights if they do their duty. Then they do not have to demand rights... This is a paramount law and no one can Change it. If Hindus consider Muslims their brothers and treat them well, Muslims too will return friendship for friendship... The duty of the Hindus is to share with the Muslims in their joys and sorrows." Gandhi then talked at some length about how each person must assume responsibility for stopping the conflict and then ended his speech by returning to its main theme: "People should not merely run after rights. He who runs after rights does not secure them. His plight is that of a dog who sees his reflection in the water and wants to attack it. His right is illusory, when you do your duty the rights will drop into your lap." (CWMG 88: 236-38).

Gandhi also said: "It is a duty of those who have realized the awful evil of the system of Indian Government to be disloyal to it and actively and openly preach disloyalty. Indeed, loyalty to a State so corrupt is a sin, disloyalty a virtue." Gandhi's categorical conclusion is that "Disobedience of the law of an evil state is therefore a duty" (CWMG 43:132-33).

Gandhi spoke in 1939 about what "true citizenship" meant: "In swaraj based on ahimsa people need not know their rights [as much as] it is necessary for them to know their duties. There is no duty but creates a corresponding right, and those only are true rights which flow from a due performance of one's duties. Hence rights of true citizenship accrue only to those who serve the State to which they belong. And they alone can do justice to the rights that accrue to them. Everyone possesses the right to tell lies. But the exercise of such a right is harmful both to the exerciser and society(CWMG 69:52). His idea of rights is moulded within the framework of Dharma: "Having a right surely does not mean that I should exercise that right in utter disregard of my sense of proportion... The exercise of right depends on one's sense of duty. It is my duty to follow dharma... I do what I consider my duty" (CWMG 69:208).

Perhaps Gandhi's emphasis on social responsibility was excessive. Parekh argues that Gandhi so restricted the roles of kama (sensual pleasure) and artha (property) in life that he "thus made dharma the sole basis of life" (Parekh, 1989 : 210). From this viewpoint, his ideas can be seen as invoking guilt and unnecessary suffering. On the other hand, as Parekh also observes, Gandhi's theory of obligation "gave a new and deeper meaning" to the current conception of our political and social nature, by extending a citizen's duties "far beyond those based on consent, promise, contract and membership of a specific community" (Ibid., 197). Through his campaigns against untouchability and for Hindu-Muslim unity, "he shamed and mobilized the Hindu masses, stirred their consciences, awakened their sense of responsibility..." (Ibid., 291).

Gandhi's theory of obligation "gave a new and deeper meaning" to the current conception of our political and social nature, by extending a citizen's duties "far beyond those based on consent, promise, contract and membership of a specific community" (Dalton 1998). Gandhi's position is that civil rights and liberties must be grounded in a prior sense of civic duty. If not, they may either remain dormant among an ignorant and apathetic population or assume a dangerous attitude in a democracy.

Excessive emphasis on social responsibilities by restricting the roles of kama (sensual pleasure) and artha (property) in life and making "dharma the sole basis of life" (Parekh 1989) is looked upon with disapproval. From the perspective of liberal democracy, Gandhi has deflated human rights theory or denied natural rights doctrine by insisting that rights exist only as derivative from performance of duty.

Gandhi believed that if each person performed his duty in accordance with the principles of Dharma and in recognition of human inter-connectedness, rights shall follow. Even though Gandhi is known as one of the prominent champions of human rights, his pursuit of the rights of Indians itself was couched in a language of duty rather than rights. He also believed that rights secured through violence was a burden on the beneficiaries.

Gandhi sought the justice that was missing in the British colonial rule over India, in the Hindu treatment of the untouchables, in the relationships between Hindu and Moslem Indians, and in the apartheid of South Africa. What Gandhi relied on for the effectiveness of this experiential working-out of justice was the fact that human beings see other human beings as other selves, that is, an identification takes place, based on the *Tat tvamasi,* the understanding of the underlying inter-identity and connectedness of all beings.

Judith Brown says:

> Those who would appropriate him for the cause of human rights fail to understand that his goal for humanity was very different from theirs, as was his perception of what was of most value in human existence. For them rights are the devices for protecting core values and attributes of individual and group life, vis a vis the forces of state and society. For him recognition of individual duty and social and moral independence were the foundation of an authentic human existence (2006 :251).

In sum, for Gandhi, rights come as part of a package together with duties (Parel, 2006) and to separate them would be not only artificial but also not beneficial to citizens. Privileging duty over rights was like privileging means over ends for Gandhi. He wanted to drive home the idea that it is after all mutual obligations that sustain the social order rather than mutual claims. In such an order obligations are fulfilled not under any compulsion, but through a process of internalization of a sense of duty without surrendering a person's individuality. Gandhi showed that one can cultivate a sense of duty without being a collectivist in the strict sense of the term.

References

Brown, Judith M (2006): "Gandhi and Human Rights in Search of True Humanity" in Richard L Johnson (Ed.). *Gandhi's Experiments with Truth: Essential Writings by a*nd about Gandhi, Lanham, MD: Lexington Books.

Dalton, Dennis(1998), "Gandhi on Freedom, Rights and Responsibility", paper presented at the International Conference of Gandhi and Twenty- First Century,

New Delhi, 30 January-4 February, available from http://www.mkgandhi.org/articles/freedom.htm accessed on 20 February 2017.

Gandhi M K, (1958-1994) *The Collected Works of Mahatma Gandhi* (CWMG), 100 Volumes, New Delhi: Publications Division.

Iyer, Raghavan (1983): The Moral and Political Thought of Mahatma Gandhi, Santa Barbara: Concord Grove.

Locke, John (1980): Second Treatise of Government, IV, 22, 1980, p. 17.

Moyn, Samuel (2016): "Rights vs. Duties: Reclaiming civic Balance" Boston Review, May 16 available from http://bostonreview.net/books-ideas/samuel-moyn-rights-duties.

Nozick, Robert (1974): Anarchy, State and Utopia, New York: Basic Books.

Parel, Anthony (2006): Gandhi's Philosophy and the Quest for Harmony, Cambridge: Cambridge University Press.

Parekh B (1989): Gandhi's Political Philosophy: A Critical Examination, Notre Dame: University of Notre Dame Press.

Porat, Benjamin (2015)"Rights-Based Law v. Duty-Based Law: Old Dilemma, New Perspective (November 28, 2015). Hebrew University of Jerusalem Legal Research Paper No. 16-04. Available at SSRN: https://ssrn.com/abstract=2696463 or http://dx.doi.org/10.2139/ssrn.2696463.

Rawls, John (1971): A Theory of Justice, Cambridge, MA: Harvard University Press.

Roberts, Christopher NJ (2015): The Contentious History of the International Bill of Human Rights, New York: Cambridge University Press.

Sri Aurobindo (1966): The Spirit and Form of Indian Polity, Calcutta: Arya Publishing.

4

Human Rights and Liberal Tradition: Theoretical Perspectives

—*K.S. Pavithran*

The history of humanity is marked by the preservation of fundamental freedoms and equality. It was also the struggle against social, economic and political oppression and against injustice and inequalities. The ideals concerning social life and the desirable structure of the society have been conceived by the enlightened humans and movements in the course of history. The ideals and convictions emanated from historical experience evolved into theory by philosphers and revolutionaries at all times. Viewed thus, it was Einstein who said that, "a large part of history is replete with the struggle for human rights, an eternal struggle in which a final victory can never be won. But to tire in that struggle would mean the ruin of society"[1].

The concept of human rights is based on the assumption that, human beings are born equal in dignity and basic rights. Contemporary human rights are considered as a universal[2] set of principles which seek to protect the equal worth of each individual human being. These principles are always applicable to all people at all time and on all places. These are basically claims which are inherent in every human being by virtue of their humanity alone. These rights enable human beings to fully use their intelligence and capabilities to satisfy their human needs. Thus ideological development, the social, economic and political content and implications and the legal status of human rights in the present day world is of paramount importance to both theorists and activists. Consequently, human rights became a buring issue and have a great significance in the modern world, especially in underdeveloped and developing nations.

A political philosophy of human rights is not a moral philosophy of human rights. It is necessarily eclectic. To grasp human rights is to engage seriously with historical, legal, idological, political as well as moral phenomena.[3] However, the Universal Declaration of Human Rights by the United Nations on 10th December 1948.[4] captured international concern for human rights. It was the first international document which proclaimed "universal respect for and observance of human rights and fundamental freedom for all without distinction as to race, sex, language or religion".[5] The United Nations Centre for Human Rights perceived human rights as "those rights which are inherent in our nature without which we cannot live as human beings.[6] Thus it is a universal and legal concept and is the basic minimum requirement for survival of human being in society.

The discourse on human rights may be a relatively modern creation but the ideas can be traced back from the ancient times. The roots of protection of rights of man can be traced from the famous 'Cyrus Cylinder', of Cyrus the greatest during the 6th Century B.C, which ensured freedom of religious practice and abolition of slavary, is considered as the first human rights document in history. Later, Babylonian king Hammurabi, issued a set of laws to his people called Hammurabi's Code. It establishes fair wages and offered protection of property. Ancient and classical philosophers contributed to this discourse in different ways. Greek and Roman thinkers recognised the idea of 'natural law' and 'natural rights'. It was asserted that these were certain rights anterior to society which too were superior to rights created by humans. Since these rights were of universal application and were supposed to have existed even before the birth of political society, they could not be violated by state.

Philosphers and political theorists are conceptualised human rights in various ways. Western philosophical tradition manifests from the ancient times, the inevitable conflict between the concept of individual rights and state authority. The great Greek playwright, Sophocles (495-406 BC) was one of the first to promote the idea of freedom of expression of opinion against the State. He stood for individual's right to resistance against the state sponsored atrocities. Plato (427-348 BC), developed an early version of universalism in ethical standards implying fair treatment to all persons, whether they are citizen or not. He made a symbiotic attempt to protect the citizens and non-citizens under a scheme of justice.

The earliest notions of 'natural rights' can be traced in the writing of philosophers like Aristotle (384-322 BC), who discussed the importance of virtue, justice and rights in accordance with the political community. Rights were secured by the Romans by the '*jus civile.*' of the Roman law. According to Roman jurist Ulpian, natural law was that "which nature and state assures to all human being"[7]. Cicero (106-43 BC) provided the philosophical foundations of later theories of natural law. He believed that there should be a universal human rights laws that transcend customery and civil laws.

In England, in 17th Century William Blackstone argued for the superiority of natural laws over man made laws. In his 'Commentaries on the Laws of England', he identified three rights – the right to personal security, right to personal liberty and private property – which have been founded on nature and reason. Another jurist A.V. Dicey argued that rights – to personal freedom, freedom of discussion and the right to assembly – were derived from the Rule of Law. The works of Thomas Aquinas (1225-1274) reflected the eternal and inalienable rights of human beings, which are validated according to Natural Law. Aquinas based his arguments on his understanding of Christian faith.

The Dutch jurist Hugo Grotius (1583 – 1645), made the first significant case for the establishment of international law to protect all citizens of the world from wars and other calamities. Grotious attempted to seperate the natural law from the thestic connections and tried to make it a part of secular rational thought.[8] He argued that it was possible to rationalise the existance of natural law and to him natural law was the basis of all positive law or written law. Further, Grotius ascertained that by the application of 'right reason', rules did not depend on any superior force (God) for its validity. The Grotian position on natural law was prevalent during the 17th century and it got transfered into natural rights. Individual rights was thus deriving straight from the natural right theory which subsequently conditioned the debate over the questions of rights during the 17th and 18th centuries.

The source of the concept of human rights can also be traced to the emergance of classical liberalism which exposed the ideas of natural inalienable, inherent fundamental rights of the individual. The concept of natural right as a pre-condition for human development received its impetus in the works of Social Contratualists – Hobbes, Locke and Rousseau. However, their premises and conclusions were remarkably different but all the three believed that the state as an institution is the most effective instrument for protecting the rights of the individual.

Thomas Hobbes (1588-1679), in his 'Leviathan' (1651) elaborates the nature of humans as essentially greedy and violent and the state of nature is with chaos and anarchy. Men in such a state are continually in competition for honour and power resulting in envy, hatred and war. Men in order to protect themselves and to get out of this desperate situation came together to establish a set of rules. This is possible because men happen to be a creature of passion, imagination, reason and will. Reason teaches them to obey natural laws, which Hobbes describes as the doctrine of Civil Society. In the absense of the idea of common good and in the light of individual good, humans entering into a contract inorder to live in peace through consent and reason. Since humans had an innate right to security from the State, they yield their natural freedom and liberty to an authority-Leviathan.

By making Leviathan all powerfull, Hobbes not only makes an absolute state but by accepting it as an artificial creation, it is also a powerful statement of individualism and there is an equality of all individuals.[9] For Hobbes the right to security was the most important human right, and he aimed at developing a Leviathan like state that could be powerful enough to protect the individuals from anarchy. Hobbes is considered to be one of the early modern thinkers to attribute to the very notion of rights. However, his negative identification of rights, as it failed to consider co-relative right of others made him an anti-humanist.

It was John Locke (1632-1704) who first argued that there are natural rights and they are inalienable and beyond the jurisdiction of any political authority. Locke's 'Second Treatise on Civil Government'(1690) articulated the idea that all human being have a state of equality by nature. Different from Hobbes, he points out that the State of nature is a state in which men are equal and free to act as they think fit within the boundary of the law of nature. From this natural law man derives natural rights – right to life, liberty and property.[10] The social contract will protect the people in the state of nature from violations. Men in the state of nature, according to Locke, created a contract to enter into a civil society. It is a contract in which man give up some and not all of the rights they possessed in the state of nature. It is a contract of all with all for protecting and preserving the rights. The resultant state must be founded on the consent and must be a constitutional state in which men acknowledged the rule of law. So it is limited and unlike in Hobbes, not absolute. Here, state exists to enlarge freedom and it is a liberal state.

Lockes doctrine of natural rights, was influenced by the Judeo-Christian tradition of protecting our rights and those of others, falls on us as individuals. He thus used the idea of rights as an attack on the idea of strong state.[11] Unlike the earlier thinkers, Locke's theory had a direct bearing on empowering the individual. The Lockean theory reiterated that the individual was an autonomous being capable of exercising choice and that more importantly he indirectly emphasised that the legitimacy of a state depends not only on the will of the people, but also upon the government's willingness and capacity to protect the natural rights of the individuals.

The Lockean proposition had a profound impact on the subsequent theoretical formulations of a good number of thinkers, who constructed the very same proposition from different stand points.A linkage of Locke's philosophy of natural law and the political constitution of states came with the publication of 'Rights of Man' by Thomas Paine (1737-1809). He was a supporter of revolutions in France and America and believed in the sovereignty of the individual. Like Locke, Paine justified his defence of certain inalienable rights – rights of mind and rights of personal happiness and freedom.

Later on, the Swiss Philospher and the prophet of French enlightenment Jean Jaques Rousseau (1712-1778) extended the social contract tradition by incorporating the idea of community with individualism. His famous observation in the 'Social Contract', that "man is born free but everywhere is in chains" was dedicated to exploring the basic condition for man to develop. His concept of 'General Will' aims common good based on equality and the General Will of the people must be represented by the community. Rousseau believed that freedom could not be achieved through anonymous states, in which democracy meant only occassional participation in the election of representatives but through smaller communities in which participatory democracy could be practiced. However, Rousseau risks imposing the general will on individuals, thus violating their individual autonomy.[12] Rousseau's theory had a direct bearing and role in setting the meaning and implications of French Revolution. Rousseaus's contemporary Voltaire called for the abolition of torture and degrading punishments. He attacked censorship by calling for a respect for freedom of opinion and expression. Similarly, Montesque's concept of the separation of powers also had a positive impact in the development and protection of human rights against state power.

It is the German philosopher Immanuel Kant (1724-1804), who is often credited with laying the ground work for modern understanding of the human rights as ethical practice.[13] For Kant the sole incontrovertible right is right to freedom. Kant provides a useful and important contribution to the human rights discourses of practical moral action by recognising fundamental human dignity. He believed in the oneness of human race and right to communal possession of earths surface by each individual. He said by virtue of all human beings are entitled to certain inalienable rights. Kant based his belief in justice on what he termed the categorical imperative of moral action which is based on three formulae – the formula of universality, the formula of the end in itself and the formula of the Kingdom of ends. The formula of universality states that morality must be impartial and non arbitrary and must involve equality. The formula of end in itself emphasises that humans should always be treated as ends in themselves and never as means to ends. The formula of Kingdom of ends demands that individuals recognise their responsibilities and affairming that morality must involve freedom. Kant made it clear that human rights were distinct from those civil rights accorded to citizens of a state by the government of that state. He provides a means for justifying human rights as the basis for self determination grounded within the authority of human reason. Thus Kant remains highly prominent in contemporary philosohphical justifications of human rights. However, Habermas critically remarked that Kant's and Rousseau's notions of autonomy are limited by the philosophy of the subject. Kant has an account of individual autonomy, but he does not have an adequate account of the relations among subjects and of how individuals come together to make the law. Rousseau to Habermas, has an account of collective autonomy and law making but risks imposing the general will on individuals thus violating their individual autonomy.[14]

The western liberal tradition of rights that are developed in the line by accepting the universality of natural law was criticised by thinkers of the same tradition. Chief among these are the Utilitrian critique of rights and the radical critique by Karl Marx. The Utilitarians, particularly Jeremy Bentham (1748-1832), has categorically negated the idea of natural law and its tag of 'universality' as meaningless.[15] Human rights and law to him are not based on any pre-social rights and law. On the contrary they are very much the result of conscious and rational decision makings. In his perspective, justice and rights are nothing but derivatives of interest and desire. There is nothing 'eternal' and 'universal' or 'pre-social' naturalness associated with them. For Utilitarians, as opposed to Kantians, qualities such as goodness or truth can only be measured in context, ie., in specific real situations, and not against any kind of abstract universal principle. Bentham's Utilitarian approach is therefore empiricist and positivist in contrast to the rationalism of his predecessors.[16]

Karl Marx (1818-1883) was also critical of the natural theory of rights. To Marx, the natural theory of right is nothing but an instrument for the bourgeoise to consolidate their rights in society. He stated that, there are no pre-social rights, since we become people only in society. Thus rights are social and political, and are achieved through historical development and struggle. Under this permise he dismissed the individualism of the Declaration of the Rights of Man in France.[17] He argued that in a class divided society, where the ownership of the means of production belongs to few, the concept of universal human rights or natural rights is nothing but, ahistorical and utopian. In a society in which Capitalists monopolise the means of production, he regarded the notion of individual rights as a bourgeois illusion. Concepts such as law, justice, morality, democracy, freedom and so on were considered as historical categories, whose content is determined by the material conditions and the social circumstances of a people. As the conditions of life change, so the content of notions and ideas may change. This is because, capitalist societies, driven by market economy, characterised by distinctions of social class – the bourgeasie, in all practicality exploiting the protectariat. The writings of Marx have resulted in various interpretations, however all of them has illuminated the exploiting nature of capitalism.

The evolution of human rights in the Western politico-philosophical tradition is deeply connected with the ideas of liberal humanism and universalism. The ideal manifestation of this fact discerned in the writings of John Rawls (1921-2002). In Rawl's theory of distributive justice, all social primary goods such as liberty and opportunity, income and wealth are to be distributed equally, unless an unequal distribution in effect become effective to the disadvantaged sections of society. For Rawls, Liberty is the pre-eminent right and that all other rights are subsidiary to it. He says, "... these rights do not depend on any particular comprehensive moral doctrine or philosphical conception of human nature.. but basic human rights express a minimum standard of well ordered political institutions for all peoples who belong, as members of good standing, to just political society of peoples".[18] Rawls further admits that human rights are a special class of rights designed to play a special role in a reasonable law of peoples for the present age. They are clearly distinct from constitutional rights, or the rights of the democratic citizenship, or from other kinds of rights that belong to political institutions.

Jurgen Habermas (b.1929) is another thinker who articulated the separation of 'universality' from natural law. To him, development of the theory of human rights forms clearly a part of the post-modern agenda. He believed that human rights and the principles of popular sovereignity constitute the 'social ideas that can justify modern laws'. Thus for Habermas, the substance of human rights resides in the formal conditions for the legal-institutionalisation of those discursive processes of opinion and will-formation in which the sovereignty of the people assumes a binding character[19] divides society into 'system' and 'life world' where the former is integrated through instrumental-strategic action and the latter through communicative action.

Habermas's theory of modernity as 'competing projects' is of great relevance in the present day context. He understand modernity to be a tension between competing forms of rationalisation, one of which is located in instrumental reason and articulated through the economic and political spheres (the 'system'), the other of which is located in communicative reason and articulated through the social cultural and personal dimensions (the 'life world'). While the former has been dominant, the latter has been ever-present as its antithesis. Human Rights are best understood as articulations of this latter modernity, given greater force after 1945, during an era of Globalisation and can provide a powerful alternative to the dominant systemic Globalisation, the global market place.[20]

To conclude, although the contemporary notion of human rights has many antecedents, both philosophical and political, it is primarily a legacy of liberalism as a political concept. More than a millennium of western history can be traced back as the background of the development of the notion of human rights. The western ideas of natural law and natural rights were conceived in a particular socio-political context of oligarchy and feudalism. However, the contributions of great minds from Plato to Habermas paved way for philosophical and scientific explorations in conceptualising human rights. The Hobbesian assault on the divine basis of 'natural rights', Locke's doctrine of limited government, Rousseau's view on social contract based on the protection of rights of each citizen, Kantian notion of the 'universality of state law based on eqality and freedom', Rawls theory of justice and Habermas's view on universality and modernity are all considered as the defining moments in this trajectory of human rights. Besides, the Utilitarian critique of natural rights, Marxian views on natural law and natural rights, in the context of *laissez faire* deserves much attention. Nevertheless, the concept of human rights cannot be viewed merely in terms of a history of ideas, it also need to be traced as emerging out of the struggles of human beings against power and oppression. Thus the idea of human rights are socially constructed in various periods of history and are changeable and contestable in the modern world.

Notes and References:

1. Einstein Albert (1954), *Ideas and Opinions*, Trans; Sonja Bargmann, Bonaza Books, p. 187.
2. Noted Post Colonial thinker Homi K. Bhabha, credits the 'universality' of human rights to the Liberal tradition. He says, liberalism has often emerged from a set of philosophies and values that are Western and European. "At the same time, it has a certain universalism and we can see the uses of it in say, human rights........", Kennth Rosario, 'A Populist Nationalism is now Alive', Interview with Homi. K. Bhaba, *The Hindu*, September17, 2017.
3. Vincent, Andrew (2010), *The Politics of Human Rights*, New York, Oxford University Press.
4. Forty eight countries voted in favour, none against, with eight-Byelorussian SSR; Czechoslovakia; Poland; Saudi Arabia; Ukranian SSR; USSR; South Africa and Yugoslovia- abstentions.
5. See, *UN General Assembly Resolution* 217A (III).
6. Alston, P. (1992), *The United Nations and Human Rights: A Critical Appraisal*, Oxford, Clarendan Press.
7. Quoted in Byrne, Darren O. (2007), *Human Rights: An Introduction*, New Delhi, Pearson Education.
8. Yasin, Adil-ul and Archana Upadhyay, (2004), *Human Rights,* New Delhi, Akansha Publishing House.
9. Yasin and Upadhyay *op. cit*., 2004.
10. Shestack, Jerome J. (2002), The Philosophical Foundations of Human Rights, in Janusz Symonides, *Human Rights: Concept and Standards*, UNESCO, Jaipur, Rawat Publications.
11. Byrne, *op.cit.,* p. 31.
12. Thomasson, Lasse (2006), Jurgen Habermas, in Terral Carver & Jannes Martin (eds), *Continental Political Thought*, Hound Mills, UK Palgrave MacMillan.
13. See, Immanuel Kant (1959) *Foundations of Metaphysics of Morals*, Indiana Polis: Bobbs-Merrill.
14. See, Jurgen Habermas (1996), '*Between Facts and Norms: Contributions to a Discouse Theory of Law and Democracy*', Trans. W. Rehg, Cambridge, MA:MIT Press.
15. Ghosal, Sarbani Guha (2010), 'Human Rights: Concept and Contestation', *The Indian Journal of Political Science*, Vol LXXI(4), Oct-Dec, p. 1107.
16. Byrne, *op. cit.,* p. 34.
17. For an elaborate study on these, see, Karl Marx (1843) ' On the Jewish Question' in *Karl Marx: Selected Writings*, David Maclallan ed., Oxford University Press, Oxford, 1977.
18. Rawls, John (2002),The Law of Peoples, in Belgrade Cirlce(ed) and Obrad Savi introduced *The Politics of Human Rights*, Verso, London & New York, pp. 31-33.

19. Habermas, Jurgen (2002) *Private and Public Autonomy*, in Belgrade Circle (ed) as cited above, pp. 60-64.
20. Byrne, *op.cit.*, p 390; A similar view has been presented by Leslie Sklair (2002), *Globalisation: Capitalism and its Alternatives*, Oxford University Press.

5

Rhetoric, Reality and the need for Inclusive Human Rights

—Sudha Mohan

Human rights are holistic and therefore need to be perceived in a more comprehensive manner than it has been hitherto. The idea has to be woven into the social fabric of life at all levels. It also has to be viewed as vehicle for human solidarity for they are claims that all people are entitled to make and the obligations and responsibilities that all people share. This paper is an attempt to underline the connections and interrelated dynamics between these three very important pillars of human transformation, namely human rights, human development and human security. The paper argues that human right which is an intrinsic, inalienable, indivisible right, to have relevance, has to be linked to human development and human security. If not, it would only be a rhetorical ideal worthy of encapsulating in theory, documents and reports with little connect to everyday lives of individuals.

Introduction

Human rights are rights inherent to all human beings, whatever our nationality, place of residence, sex, national or ethnic origin, colour, religion, language, or any other status. We are all equally entitled to our human rights without discrimination. These rights are all inter-related, interdependent and indivisible." (UDHR: 1948). Human rights express our deepest commitment to ensure that all persons are secure in their enjoyment of the goods and freedoms that are necessary for dignified living. The Universal Declaration of Human Rights, signed on December 10, 1948, thus, transformed an aspiration into legally binding standard and initiated a number of institutions to scrutinise government conformity and condemn noncompliance.

The fundamental idea of human development, which believes in enriching the lives and freedoms of ordinary people, has much in common with the concerns expressed by various declarations of human rights. Human development is the process of enlarging people's choices, by expanding human functioning's and capabilities. Human development therefore reflects human outcomes in these functioning's and capabilities. It represents a process as well as an end. It focuses on improving the lives of people. It is about giving people more freedom and opportunities to live lives they value. In effect this means developing people's abilities and giving them a chance to use them. Three foundations for human development are to live a healthy and creative life, to be knowledgeable, and to have access to resources needed for a decent standard of living. UNDP 2001). One of the main objectives of human development is to create opportunities for all people to implement their own choices, participating in the development process, particularly in those issues impacting on their lives and interests, enjoyment of freedoms. Human development is about people, about expanding their choices to lead their lives they value. (Selim Jahan: 2002). Thus, the promotion of human development and the fulfilment of human rights undoubtedly share a common motivation.

The term "human security" was introduced into international discussion in the 1990s as a response to new (or more generalized) "downside risks" that could affect everyone. The United Nations Development Programme (UNDP: 1994) defined human security as both "safety from such chronic threats as hunger, disease and repression" and protection from sudden and hurtful disruptions in the patterns of daily life" (United Nations Development Programme 1994, 23) Although the actual term "human security" was first used by the UNDP in 1994, its origins can be traced to earlier UN commissions on the environment, development, and global governance. (Gerd Oberleitner 2005). Human security is a conceptual shift towards putting the human being in the centre as well as an operational tool to conceptualise policy. (Mohan Sudha 2007). Definitions of human security range from a broad concept, which is concerned with the well-being of individuals to a narrower concept of protection from a certain number of violent threats. Kofi Annan (2000) has observed: Human security in its broadest sense, embraces far more than the absence of violent conflict. It encompasses human rights, good governance, access to education and health care and ensuring that each individual has opportunities and choices to fulfil his or her potential.

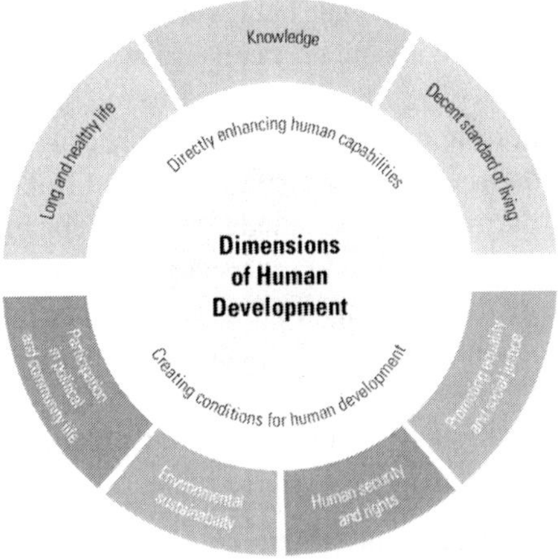

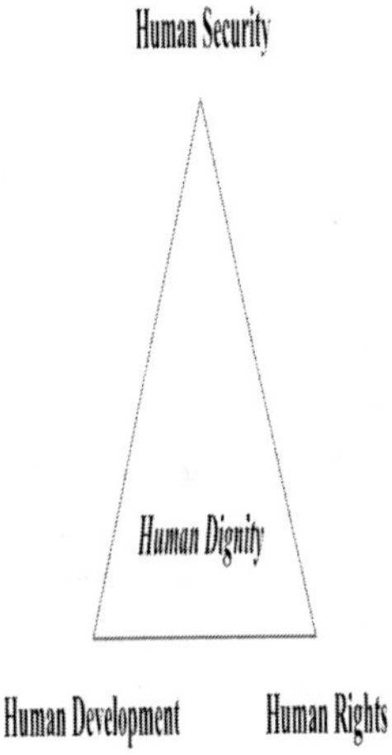

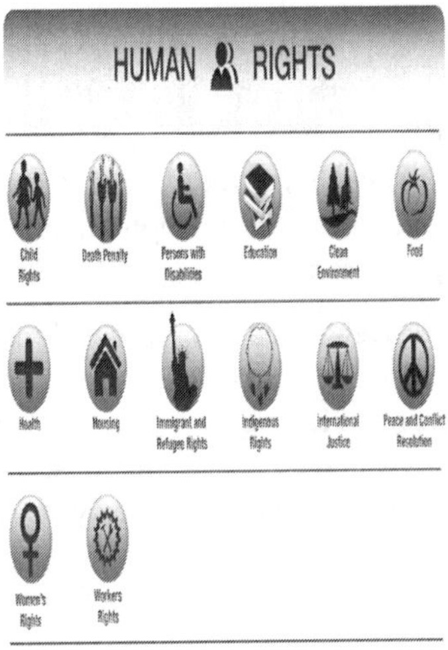

The first figure highlights the dimensions of Human Development, the third various types of human rights and right holders and the second is a diagrammatic representation of the symbiotic representation that views these three in an inter-related, inter-related triangle.

Linkages and interconnections between Human rights, human development and human security

Human rights, human development and human security are all human focused and hold human beings at the centre of the universe. Human rights form the core and normative foundation of human security, which also is intricately linked to concerns of human development. However, scholars from different discipline of social sciences have been raising the question whether one or which one should take precedence over the other? This particular paper attempts to understand the symbiotic relationships between the three and argues that none should take precedence over the other. All the three are central to not only our understanding of rights but also policies of development and security. This paper also argues that these triumvirates need to be linked for a better theoretical understanding as well as for considering their practical implications for human wellbeing.

As such, it is understood that rights, development and security are three pillars of human beings, which are recognized in international human rights instruments. The Universal Declaration of Human Rights (UDHR 1948) for instance, proclaims that "Everyone is entitled to all the rights and freedoms set forth in this Declaration... and "has the right to life, liberty and security of person." As a principle provided in international human rights law, states have the duty to respect for, protect and fulfil human rights for all without distinction on the grounds indicated in international human rights treaties.

Human rights and human development are explicitly expressed in former Secretary-General Kofi Annan's statement as "integrated blocks of human security". He highlights the inter-relationship of rights, development and security whereby development, security and human rights go hand in hand; no one of them can advance very far without the other two. He also claimed how it is imperative to voice on all three issues to ensure that freedom from want, freedom from fear and freedom to live in dignity carry real meaning for those most in need. (Anan Kofi 2006).

The Human rights (HR) discourse to transcend beyond the 'discourse' to have meaning and relevance to everyday life and living, has to be juxtaposed along with Human Development (HD) and Human Security (HS). The following diagram clearly depicts the interconnection between the three pillars.

From: Security Edited by: Mary Martin, Taylor Owen 2013

Human development is a broader concept, which is defined as a process of widening the range of people's choices; while human security means that people can exercise these choices freely and safely and that they can relatively confident that the opportunities they have today are not totally lost tomorrow. As such, progress in one area enhances progress in the other, but failure in one area also heightens the risk of failure in the other. (UNDP, 1994)

Amartya Sen's work offers a succinct theoretical discussion of the relationship between development and human rights. Development, in his view, is to be understood as the progressive expansion of individual freedoms (Sen 1999: 19). This includes the elimination of economic deprivation, as well as requiring an individual's voice in the political decision-making process and in development itself. Human rights are thus an intrinsic aspect of development. At the same time, Sen emphasises that individual freedoms contribute instrumentally to development. Hence development and human rights are to be understood as two sides of the same coin. The right to development, enshrined by a General Assembly Declaration in, provides a good example of this amalgamation of development and human rights: it has been described as a 'vector' of human rights, as well as a human right in itself. (OCHR 2001 and UNDP 1998). Inequality, Deprivation and Poverty is a violation of HRs just as slavery, torture leading to brutally inhumane and unjust social order. Therefore, freedom from poverty is a human right, as made clear in the Universal declaration of Human Rights.

It is important here to mention that human rights are supposed to encompass certain "soft rights" such as the right to education or freedom from poverty and "hard rights" which fall under criminal law, such as the right not to be tortured. (Blau and Moncada 2016). Also, Bryan Turner, in Vulnerability and Human rights, (1993) argues that all humans are vulnerable at some point in their lives, providing a universal basis for human rights. This issue was central in the commission of Human Security report whereby it defines human security as: "...to protect the vital core of all human lives in ways that enhance human freedoms and human fulfilment. Human security means protecting fundamental freedoms–freedoms that are the essence of life. It means protecting people from critical (severe) and pervasive (widespread) threats and situations. It means using processes that build on people's strengths and aspirations. It means creating political, social, environmental, economic, military and cultural systems that together give people the building blocks of survival, livelihood and dignity." (CHS: 2003: 4)

Human Rights and Human Security are therefore both "essentially a manifestation of human dignity" (Nowak 2003:1). Human dignity is also a fundamental concept of human security. Human Security places a premium on human dignity. The toleration of human rights violations for the sake of economic development or social stability has no place in the human security paradigm. (Acharya 2001: 45). Another leading specialist in the human rights field, Bertrand G. Ramacharan,(2002) also points out that human rights define human security. This implies that a human right itself also encompasses human security. For individuals and entire communities at large, in order for them to enjoy the right to life, food, housing, education, participation, etc. it cannot help without saying about security factors. The threats to security listed were deliberately chosen to reflect seven distinct categories of human insecurity (health, food, economic, personal, community, political and environmental) and to show that the concept being proposed was "all-encompassing" and directed towards "freedom from fear" as well as "freedom from want" (UNDP 1994: 24). This definition of security was therefore "people-centered" and "universal", and consisted of "interdependent" components.

Human development approach is to place human beings at the central part of the development process. Hence, when one mentions the expanding of opportunities for human beings to participate in the development process, it is synonymous to emphasize on the equality or "growth with equity". (CHS 2003). Nevertheless, there is nothing to guarantee that, even in a highly developed society, people are not subjected to vulnerability created by them and brought in by the development process itself, depriving opportunities away from participating and implementing their fundamental freedoms. (IPCC 2007) Swift economic development, for instance, may lead to environmentally unsustainable development, creating the risk to livelihoods of future generations. (Korten 2002). In other words, people may be subjected to consequences brought about by the negative side of development. Globalization, increased trade liberalization, inappropriate exploitation of natural resources, for instance, can be considered as catalysts causing such risks. It is in this context that human security counts. Human security is to protect human fundamental freedoms, to shield people from vulnerabilities. More specifically, it aims to protect people from risks that they may face in their daily lives that deter their development as well as enjoyment of their rights.

Failed or limited human development leads to a backlog of human deprivation – poverty, disease, hunger or persisting disparities between ethnic communities or between regions, and as consequence this backlog in access to power and economic opportunities can lead to violence. So, as Jakkie Cilliers (2002: 12) contends that "if human development is freedom from want (a process of widening the range of people's choices), human security can be understood as the ability to pursue those choices in a safe environment and on an equal basis with others. Human development contributes to human security by tackling the long-term structural causes of conflict and by strengthening the capability of societies to deal with conflict in a peaceful manner.

Like rights and security, development and security go hand in hand with each other. For instance, insecurity due to violence or deprivation prevents development. Development in turn brings in opportunities and better conditions for individuals to realize their freedoms. In other words, development, on the one hand, enable individuals to materialize and bring into play their potentials, while security, on the other hand, aims to protect people from risks in the development process and to implement their fundamental freedoms. Human rights are violated not only by terrorism, repression or assassination but also by unfair economic structures that create huge disparities.

Thus, human development, human security and human rights are pillars aimed at ensuring the life quality, enabling people to realize and bring into play their potentials, at the same time protecting people from vulnerabilities arising in their daily lives. These three pillars have a supplementary relationship, like a tripod model. Where one of the three pillars is absent, the other two find them hardly standing firmly on their own foots, and individual survival is threatened.

Taken all together, human rights and human security can be fruitfully supplementary one to another. Though the human rights framework is more basic and more fundamental due to its legal basis as well as enforcement mechanisms, there are gaps left by the normative nature of the concept of human rights, especially when it comes up with the question of which particular freedoms are crucial enough to count as human rights that society should acknowledge, safeguard and promote, and this is where human security can support and supplement human rights. (Sen 2003). However, it is also important to point out briefly the issues and problems related to the violation of human rights that are intricately linked to the both development and security concerns. The following section will make an attempt to examine these concerns.

Infringement of Human Right

Inequality, Deprivation and Poverty is a violation of Human Right: Just as slavery, torture and violence lead to vicious and inhuman and unjust social order, deprivation is also a human right abuse. Therefore, freedom from poverty is a HR, as made clear in the Universal declaration of Human Rights. Thus the following statistics will clearly highlight how deprivation, poverty and inequality and primarily economic insecurities can heighten vulnerabilities and undermine the tenets of HRs and make it a rhetorical and not a real right for the vast majority.

Take for example the latest Oxfam's report, (2017) aptly entitled '*An economy for the 99 percent*', shows that the gap between rich and poor is far greater than had been feared. It details how big business and the super-rich are fuelling the inequality crisis by dodging taxes, driving down wages and using their power to influence politics. It calls for a fundamental change in the way we manage our economies so that it work for all people, and not just a fortunate few. For instance, the richest 1 percent in India owns 58 percent of the country's wealth. The report also highlights that between 1988 and 2011, the incomes of the poorest 10 percent around the world increased by an average of just $65 per year, while those of the richest 1 percent grew by an average of $11,800 a year—182 times as much. Oxfam has also revealed that over the last 25 years, the top 1 percent have gained more income than the bottom 50 percent put together," says the report. Data on the distribution of global wealth – particularly in India and China

– indicates that the poorest half of the world has less wealth than had been previously thought. Nine billionaires owned the same wealth as the poorest half of the planet. Seven out of 10 people live in a country that has seen a rise in inequality in the last 30 years. (Oxfam Report 2017).

Even the latest UNDP's recent report shows how India has slipped one place from an already pathetic position of 130 to 131 among the 188 countries ranked in terms of human development. Life expectancy at birth is 68.3 years; Expected years of schooling is 11.7 years; Gross National Income (per capita) is $5,663; (UNDP online March 22, 2017). Everyone should have the right to education, health care and other basic services. Putting this principle of universalism into practice will require dedicated attention and resources particularly for the poor and other vulnerable groups said the report.

This scenario was highlighted by the UNDP Report 2014 that many global public goods have social value and can reduce vulnerability, but they are undervalued by markets. This is not only true and relevant but also resonated in 2017 as well. This statement is particularly ***compelling*** when we examine the staggering global economic inequalities and the wide disparity that primarily lead to the occupy Wall Street and other movements in the US as well as the slogan "we are the 99 percent! This has also been exacerbated by what David Harvey calls "accumulation by dispossession" wherein the acquisition of wealth through displacement of peasants, farmers and workers is on the rise almost everywhere. (Harvey 2005).

The role of Neo liberal State in undermining Human Rights, Human Security and Human Development:

The changing role of the state in India, especially since the 1990s in the context of globalisation and governance has to be linked to the ways in which its policies lead to or negates its central function of bringing about inclusive development, whether in the social, economic and ecological spheres. If the state is unable or unwilling to usher in such inclusion, it is bound to fail or succeed superficially. Governance, propped and promoted by the India has to be understood in the context of an increasingly pluralised state sharing power with multiple actors within a complex network of associations and organisations. The state also had to reckon with its own changing role and of established rules that has transformed its functions. It has become what is called as the Commodified State, where Statesmanship is transformed into Salesmanship—where the Nation State is branded as a location to globally footloose capital and firms. (Mohan 2017). Analysing human rights from a postcolonial perspective Kapoor (2006) provides an enriched perspective of how the terrain has operated and the politics of inclusion and exclusion that it has sustained and even justified. What challenges are posed to human rights -to its dark side as well as the extent to which are human rights being aligned with neo-liberalism and inclusion into the market.

Brown, (2005) argues that neo-liberalism is becoming dominant as governmentality, and may emerge as the dominant ideology, where privatisation schemes and a flourishing market economy become the measure of democracy. This formation is global though constructed through local manoeuvres such as 'corporatized media, schools and prisons. It is also a formation that is established partly through the production of a neo-liberal citizenry, where individuals are entrepreneurial actors across all dimension of their lives. Neoliberal market approach constructs citizens as consumers who exercise voice by deciding where to spend or invest their money. (Mohan 2017).

The commodification of Human Rights: Neo-liberal states unabashedly absolve itself of human responsibilities and thereby convert Human Rights as Prof. Upendra Baxi (2009) highlights the commodification of human rights. He also argues that we must halt the current human rights paradigm shift from that of the UDHR focus on human dignity and well-being, to one that focuses on global capital and corporate well being, rejecting any material redistributive role for the state. (Baxi 2009). As a consequence of this trend especially since the post cold war period, what is also witnessed is the growth of human rights entrepreneurs and technocrats who commodify and professionalize human rights discourse and human suffering in order to package and sell it according to what the markets will allow. (Baxi 2001). Human Rights are marketed to those with money to buy their 'liberty.' Most importantly, the human rights movements also organise themselves in the image of the markets, inevitably merchandizing human suffering and human rights. The brazen corporate branding of human rights is not new. Baxi (2000) also has outspokenly illuminated the limits of human rights models that are not based on an understanding of power relations and structural inequalities. He therefore called for the voices of suffering to be heard in the contemplation of human rights histories and analyses.

Thus, Baxi (2015) critiques much of the discourse and many of the current practices relating to human rights. He portrays human rights as phenomena embedded in the experiences of suffering. This, which Baxi terms "critical human rights realism," should be used as a resource for the poor and oppressed in their fight for a better life. As a scholar activist, Baxi stresses the importance of not losing touch with the experience of suffering and the needs of the poor and oppressed who, notwithstanding their exclusion, should be the main authors of human rights. Likewise, Baxi speaks of the gap between human rights discourse and the lived experiences of "culturally constituted human-ness," i.e. it is important to "humanize" human rights. Indeed, Baxi stresses that "the 'local,' not the 'global' remains the crucial locus of struggle for the enunciation, implementation, and enjoyment of human rights. (Baxi 2009)

Dehumanization of human rights occurs in the context of international investment arbitration, where the claims of firms are often articulated and adjudicated with language and standards borrowed from human rights law. This development is described as the dehumanization of human rights, is part of a larger process whereby international economic institutions accord legal recognition and certain protections to private economic actors. (Turkuler Isiksel 2016).

The article traces the important implications of business corporations being considered as bearers of human rights for determining the proper scope and purpose of international human rights norms, and for conceptualizing their relationship to constitutional democracy. Human rights are in the process of being appropriated to protect transnational corporations and bolster their claims against states. Human rights discourse has been marshalled in the context of international investment law to articulate, adjudicate, and vindicate the claims of investors with concepts, language, and standards borrowed from human rights discourse. As one observer writes, the contemporary international investment regime is thoroughly appropriationist in terms of human rights, appealing to human rights norms to buttress the rights of foreign investors, rather than the rights of individuals and communities affected by investor practices. (Perterson 2009).

Banalisation of human right, as Sashi Kumar remarks, "Gramscian hegemony, more than overt imperialism, characterises contemporary mass culture and media. A paradigm shift in the way we understand, represent and experience the world subserves a new and aggressive corporate teleology." (Sashi K 2011: 38). The media more often than not also trivialises and also participate in this process of banalising human rights. (Franc 2001) It is obvious in the manner in which minorities, indigenous peoples, immigrant populations as well as racial, religious, ethnic, gender and sexual minorities, people with disability are treated and also reported about in the media. This made the scholar Spivak Gayatri (2004) to comment that we theorise, critique, challenge and mobilise HR activity in a world that still does not share a stable universal proof that we are born free. Do these groups, mentioned above, face uncertainly as the HR debate is framed, constructed and reconstructed on the axes of recognition and redistribution dilemma? (Eleni & Goodlad: 2010). Human Rights Watch 2016 highlights serious HR violation with regards to minorities, impunity (AFSPA), women's rights, children's rights, gender and sexual rights, disability rights. In the similar vien, the Global Media Monitoring Project (GMMP) in its 2010 report stated that nearly two thirds (63 per cent) of the news stories from the Indian media that were analysed reinforced gender stereotypes while only 9 per cent challenged them. This unfortunate problem arises when the media in its own overt and covert ways supports and promotes the constructing and stereotyping content that deals with human rights and its abuse. (Mohan, Sudha 2014).

Ways to overcome the faultlines and flaws

If connectedness, inclusion and equality and reciprocity are three key features of democratic communities, then they also should be the underlying logic of HRs. It is self evident that HRs, civil and political rights, non-discrimination, the rights to a decent job, housing, education, social protections and economic security and cultural rights, must be made practical and concrete in everyday life. It is just not sufficient to have constitutional guarantees and laws, HRs need to be grounded in communities and infused throughout democratic institutions. It is also important to have not just right in the city but also right to the city. (Mohan Sudha 2017).

People's Decade for Human Rights Education and Learning is an International Consortium for Learning Human Rights as a Way of Life. As the founder of this movement pointed out, "Women and men must join in building a new political culture based on human rights through learning about the practical holistic vision of human rights. We have no other option if we are to achieve economic and social justice in equality and non-discrimination for all."- (Shulamith Koenig Recipient of the 2003)

The International Human Rights Cities programme is rooted in communities that have chosen to incorporate human rights into their everyday lives; to train and empower citizens to know their human rights in order to claim their human rights. It aims at collaboration and consensus to change the underlying values and attitudes that contribute to violence and misery Rather than an imposition, the human rights city evolves from within the community, accommodating its unique cultural norms and behaviours, and its own approaches to consensus and coalition building. The commonality in each Human Rights City is to enable "freedom from fear" and "freedom from want" within their own communities. (website ushrnetwork.org: 2017)

Importance of putting power and politics back at the center of analysis: Putting power back at the center of analysis and by recognizing struggles for rights as political struggles, then rights-based approaches can not only secure progress in realizing rights for people living in poverty, but also strive for structural change where the balance of power is tilted away from powerful elites and towards the mass of rights-deprived people.(Crawford: 2015) Mander (2005) also argues in a similar vein that an understanding of poverty as the outcome of the active denial of people's rights implies a rejection of understanding development as a neutral process, and instead an acknowledgement of its *political* content.

A spotlight on rights: by different constituencies – movement, civil society groups academic and research based organisations - that can serve as an interlocutor of the state and public policy. Thus knowledge about and emphasize on rights is very crucial. This is also closely linked to knowledge building on Human rights.

Freedom from violence: Violence against which cuts across caste, class, ethnicity and other forms of social division. Research on violence, legal activism to get laws and public policy into place, and to get help and support to victims, along with campaigns to insert this issue into the broader human rights agenda both nationally and internationally is very important.

Equal leadership: Providing Women and the marginalised sections a voice in the decisions that affect their lives. Studies have also shown how that when women become leaders in their local community, they transform the development agenda—focusing on the right to water, sanitation, health, education and nutrition, besides, combating corruption, social exclusion and domestic violence.

Economic rights, poverty and the right to social protection: An insightful account of this is examined in *Collins, et al (2009) book Portfolios of the Poor.* It is evident in several studies that that when women control money, it is far more likely to be invested in the health, nutrition and education of children than when men control the money.

Education and Functional adult literacy: Millions of women have never had the opportunity of formal education. Women are twice as likely to be non-literate as men. Literacy is more than skill acquisition; it is the reclamation of autonomous selfhood and agency (Duflo, 2012). Education can have a range of benefits within the households with short as well as long term advantages.

Access to justice: To be equal before the law and to have access to the institutions of the law in seeking justice are fundamental to democratic understanding of citizenship. However, the experience of most marginalized groups is that they have little or no access to such institutions.

Protection of individuals and groups: This is critical against power exertion, not only from states, but also from other agencies exerting power, such as transnational corporations, NGOs, and international organizations.

A focus on non-discrimination: equal opportunity and participation irrespective of race, colour, sex, language, religion, political or other opinion, national or social origin, property, birth, or other status. Participation and to some extent also non-discrimination will relate to political rights including freedom of association, assembly, and speech.

Justice that is less legal and more social - which moves part of the discourse on human rights from the courtrooms and the top-institutions to areas where there is a dire need for both protection and fulfillment of human rights.

Enabling support: This allows individuals and groups to lead a life in dignity, free of poverty, with access to certain minimum standards of living, health, water, and education. What is central here is to approach basic capabilities via human rights, including an effort to enable people to organize and to demand their rights.

In Conclusion, it is critical to note that neither the Human Development nor Human security approach does not replace but seeks to complement and build upon state security, human rights, and human development. (Mohan 2012). Should our status and position in the world affairs be commensurate with our indices in other parameters, is a question we need to ask and also answer. More importantly, we need to work out alternatives towards making human security, human rights and human development a viable and workable option that will enable freedom from want as well as fear. Human security is a concept in motion, a work in progress, evolving as it should, with new and continuously emerging human needs and threats that arise both out of personal as well as political threats. (Mohan 2012).

Thus, this paper argues that there are very strong linkages between a human development, human security paradigm and human rights. What human rights can achieve in development relates to the creation of a space of protection and dignity around the human person from where development and security can move forward. We therefore need integration of human security and human development into human rights discourse as a strategy of empowerment. This is very important because marginalisation has development security and rights dimension that is central to the living conditions of every human being in general but specifically of poor and vulnerable people in particular.

As Eleanor Roosevelt "Where, after all, do universal human rights begin? In small places, close to home – so close and so small that they cannot be seen on any maps of the world.... Unless these rights have meaning there, they have little meaning anywhere. Without concerned citizen action to uphold them close to home, we shall look in vain for progress in the larger world."

Reference

Acharya Amitav (2001). Human Security: East versus West. International Journal, Vol. 56,No. 3, Summer. 442-460.

Acharya Amitav, (2001). Constructing a Security Community in Southeast Asia ASEAN and the problem of regional order, London, NY, Routledge.

Baxi, Upendra (2001). The Future of Human Rights, Oxford: Oxford University Press.

Commission on Human Security N.Y.

Baxi Upendra, (2002). The Future of Human Rights, Oxford University Press, Oxford, 119–131.

Baxi *Upendra, Francis Deng, Abdullahi An-Na'im, Yash Ghai,* (2009). *Human Rights, Southern Voices* (William Twining ed., Cambridge Univ. Press, 157- 208.

Baxi Upendra, (2015). Human Rights Responsibility of Multinational Corporations, Political Ecology of Injustice: Learning from Bhopal Thirty Plus? Business and Human Rights Journal, 1 (2015), pp. 21–40.

Blau Judith and Alberto Moncada, (2016). Human Rights: A Primer, London and NY, Routledge.

CHS(2003)Concept of Human Security. Available at : http://www.un.org/humansecurity/sites/www.un.org.humansecurity/files/human security in_theory and practice_english.pdf

Coundouriotis Eleni & Lauren M. E. Goodlad (2010) Comparative Human Rights: Literature, Art, Politics, Journal of Human Rights, 9:2, 121-126.

Crawford Gordon, Bård A. Andreassen (2015). Human Rights and Development: Putting Power and Politics at the Center, Human Rights Quarterly, Vol. 37, Volume 37, Number 3, pp. 662-690.

Dufflo Esther. (2012). Women Empowerment and Economic Development, Journal of Economic Literature, 50(4): 1051-79.

Eleni Coundouriotis & Lauren M. E. Goodlad (2010) Comparative Human Rights: Literature, Art, Politics, Journal of Human Rights, 9:2, 121-126.

Franc, Oise Tulkens (2001). Human rights, rhetoric or reality? European Review, Vol. 9, No. 2, 125–134.

Gerd Oberleitner, (2005). Human Security: A Challenge to International Law, Global Governance. Vol. 11, No. 2, July, 185-203.

Global Media Monitoring Project, GMMP (2010) Report, 'Who Makes the News? http://whomakesthenews.org/gmmp/gmmp-reports/gmmp-2010-reports.

Gordon Crawford and Bård A. Andreassen. (2015). Human Rights and Development: Putting Power and Politics at the Center, Democracy and Human Rights Human Rights Quarterly, Volume 37, Number 3, August.

Harvey David, A brief History of Neoliberalism, (2005). Oxford, Oxford University Press.

Human Security reports available online at: http://www.un.org/humansecurity/sites/www.un.org.humansecurity/files/chs_final_report_-_english.pdf

Human Rights Cities Alliance: http://www.ushrnetwork.org/our-work/project/national-human-rights-cities-alliance.

Human Rights Watch (2016) https://www.hrw.org/world-report/2016/country-chapters/india.

Intergovernmental Panel on Climate Change (IPCC 2007) https://www.ipcc.ch/publications_and_data/publications_ipcc_fourth_assessment report_synthesis report.htm

Jakkie Cilliers, (2004). Human Security in Africa, African Human Security Initiative.

Kofi Annan, (2006). Message of the United Nations Secretary-General, on the Human Rights Day of 2006 with a theme "Fighting Poverty: A Matter of Obligation not Charity", at http://www.un.org/events/humanrights/2006/statements.shtml

Kofi Annan, (2000). Press Release SG/SM/7382, "Secretary-General Salutes International Workshop on Human Security in Mongolia.

Korten David, (1992). Getting to the 21th Century, Harford, Kumarian Press, 1991; World.

Peterson, L. E (2009). Human Rights and Bilateral Investment Treaties Investing in Human Rights, International Centre for Human Rights and Democratic Development.

Mander Harsh, "Rights as struggle – towards a more just and humane world, in: Paul Gready and Jonathan Ensor(eds.), Reinventing Development? Translating rights-based approaches from theory into practice,(London: Zed Books 2005), pp. 233-278.

Mohan, Sudha (2012). Conceptualising Human security in the Age of Globalisation" in Saurab and B. C. Upreti (Ed) Strengthening SAARC: Exploring Vistas for Expanding Co-operation. Pentagon Press, February 2012, 10-22.

Mohan, Sudha (2017). Politics of Urban Space: Rethinking Urban Inclusion and the Right to the City. In Anita Lacey (ed.) Women, Urbanization and Sustainability:

Practices of Survival, Adaptation and Resistance. Basingstoke, UK: Palgrave Macmillan: 2017, 157-178.

Mohan, Sudha (2017). State of the State: Politics of Power Shifts and Shifting Power of the State in India, Current Opinion in Environmental Sustainability 2017, 24:42–46.

Mohan, Sudha, Empowerment of Women, Media and Human Rights (2014. Journal of Human Right, National Human Rights Commission, December 2014. 151-167.

Nowak, Manfred (2007). Introduction to the International Human Rights Regime. Human Rights Law Review 7 (1): 251-259.

OHCHR RTD. (1948). Office of the High Commissioner, United Nations Human Rights). http://www.ohchr.org/EN/Issues/Pages/WhatareHumanRights.aspx

Oxfam (2017). https://www.oxfam.org/en/pressroom/pressreleases/2017-01-16/just-8-men-own-same-wealth-half-world.

Peterson, Luke (2009), 'Human Rights and Bilateral Investment Treaties: Mapping the role of human rights law within investor-state arbitration', Rights & Democracy, International Centre for Human Rights and Democratic Development, Montraeal Canada.

Ramcharan Bertrand G. (2002). Human Rights and Human Security, International studies in human rights The Hague; London : Martinus Nijhoff. Available at www.humansecurity-chs.org/activities/outreach/ramcharan.html

Ratna Kapur, (2006). Human Rights in the 21st Century: Take a Walk on the Dark Side, Sydney Law Review, 28: 665.

OHCHR (2017) Webiste for issues relating to Development and Human rights.

http://www.ohchr.org/EN/Issues/Development/Pages/DevelopmentIndex.aspx

Sashi Kumar, (2011). Hegemony in Contemporary Culture and Media and the Need for a Counter Initiative, EPW Economic & Political Weekly, December 17, xlvi no 51.

Sashi Kumar. (2014). Unmediated-Essays on Media, Culture, Cinema, Tulika Books.

Selim Jahan (2002) "Evolution of the Human Development Index," Section 2 from Handbook of Human Development", Oxford University Press.

Sen A (2003). Feminist Economics, IX,2-3, 301-317.

Sen A, (1980). Equality of What? In Tanner Lecture on Human Values, Edited by S.McMurrin, Cambridge UK, Cambridge University Press.

Sen, A.(1999): Development as Freedom, Oxford: Oxford University Press Sen, Amartya (1999) Development as Freedom, Oxford: Oxford University Press.

Shulamith Koenig Recipient of the 2003 UN Award for outstanding achievement in the field of Human Rights. Speech Available at http://www.pdhre.org/ Spivak, Gayatri Chakravorty. (2004) Righting wrongs. South Atlantic Quarterly, 103(2/3), 523–581.

Turkuler Isikse. (2016).The Rights of Man and the Rights of the Man-Made: Corporations and Human Rights. Human Rights Quarterly, Volume 38, Number 2, May, pp. 294-349.

Turner Bryne (1993). Outline of a General Theory of Human Rights, Sociology 27, No. 3. 489-512.

UDHR (1948), Article 2 and 3 of UDHR Adopted and proclaimed by the General Assembly resolution 217 A (III) of 10 December.

UNDP (1994). New dimensions of human security. Human development report. New York, Oxford: Oxford University Press [online]. Available at <http://hdr.undp.org/

UNDP (2001) United Nations Development Programme). Human Development Report. New York: Oxford University Press.

UNDP (2014) United Nations Development Programme). Human Development Report. New York: Oxford University Press.

UNDP Human Development report (2016) published in March 2017 available at http://hdr.undp.org/en/composite/HDI

UNDP Report 2017. http://hdr.undp.org/en/content/world%E2%80%99s-most-marginalized-still-left-behind-global-development-priorities-undp-report

UNDP, Human Development Report (1994) New Dimensions of Human Security (http://hdr.undp.org)

United Nations Development Programme (1998). Integrating Human Rights with Development', Report New York Oxford Oxford University Press.

Wendy Brown, (2005). Edgework: Critical Essays on Knowledge and Politics, princeton university press princeton and oxford.

6

Marketing the Environment: Environmental Rights and Corporate Environmentalism

— *Nirmala V. U.*

Introduction

Environmental movements grew out of the dissatisfaction for dominant development models and posed challenges to economic systems that preached humans as the conquerors of nature. Though the movements emerged with an elitist conservationist character it changed dimensions and acquired many forms leading to the birth of multifaceted movements. Cutting across the left and right of the political spectrum these movements mixed greens with colours ranging from red to black. Environmentalisms crossed the boundaries of left and right politics and succeeded in generating a discourse on environmental human rights. The paper intends to understand, how the varying discourse of environmental rights that questioned dominant development models was appropriated for the sustenance of the same especially the sustenance and expansion of capitalism. Or, how a critique of capitalism was appropriated by the capitalist system for its expansion?

Concern for the environment was not a new one as one can find numerous writings in this regard by a simple glance at the history of political philosophy or religious literature. Modern environmentalism mostly started as a moral critique of the industrial revolution and resultant environmental degradation. It focused on conservation of nature and wilderness (Guha 2000). But today, environmentalism is a multifaceted ideology and movement. Environmentalism as a political idea is relatively new and it got popularized in the 1960s, after the publication of Rachel Carson's book the *Silent Spring (1962)* in the USA and received global recognition through the *United Nations Conference on Human Environment* popularly known as the Stockholm Conference of 1972. The Stockholm conference led to the emergence of a global platform for addressing environmental issues viz, the UNEP. One of the major contributions of the conference was the recognition of environmental rights as the fundamental human right. The conference proclaimed that "...both aspects of man's environment natural and manmade are essential for his well being and to the enjoyment of basic human rights, the right to life itself"(UN General Assembly 1972).

But it needs to be mentioned that though such a move was made in the early 1970s itself, the idea of environment as a human right concern remained dormant for some time as the major focus of environmental movements of the North was on conservation of nature, protection of wilderness and aesthetics. It was the debates on sustainable development and the movements for environmental justice strengthened the idea of the right to environment as a human right. The sustainable development debate which got introduced in Stockholm received the attention of the world through the Brundtland Commission report (1987) and subsequent actions. Instead of focusing merely on aspects of conservation it called upon the world to conserve not simply for the sake of nature but for the present and future generations of humans. The debate brought forward the need for balancing economic development with nature. The movements for environmental justice blended the environmental questions to class, race, gender and many other issues. The Basel Declaration (1989) on the prevention of exporting toxic waste from the developed to developing nations do have a significance in this case. It incorporated the elements of justice in environmental debates. But environmental justice as an idea thrived along with the movements against the selective locations of landfills and toxic industries in the United States. The discriminatory policies of the governments and the corporates in locating these hazardous elements near black habitats were questioned by the environmental movements which brought for a discussion on the discrimination and injustice involved in distributing ill effects of environmental damages (Dobson 1998). The lack of class and racial sensitivity involved in mainstream environmental movements were raised to the forefront by these movements. Instead of conservation, wilderness and endangered species protection debates popularised by the mainstream environmentalism these new movements debated the discrimination faced by the marginalised sections of the society when it comes to the sharing of environmental benefits and adversities.

The disproportionate impact of environmental damage was brought to the fore. These movements incorporated aspects of social and distributive justice into the debates on environmental sustainability (Dobson 1998). It can be considered as an attempt to democratize the idea of environmentalism by incorporating justice components of accessibility, distribution, and decision making power related to the environment. It also needs to be mentioned that a counter-initiative namely the ecological justice debate, an eco-centric debate was also emerging in the period.

The demands for environmental justice boosted the claims for the right to environment further. Today there is a consensus regarding the case that right to environment is a basic condition for the fulfillment of many other human rights like right to life, health, water, food, and sanitation. There are also demands for considering the right to have a clean and healthy environment as a human right in itself. In short, these debates were more anthropocentric in nature and it boosted the idea of the right to environment. Right to have a quality environment was accepted as an integral part of human rights and it was incorporated as the third generation of human rights.

Capitalism in Conflict with Nature and the Role of State

Capitalism is an economic system that bases on the idea of atomized individuals. It essentially believes in the domination of nature by man. Capitalism, to the ecological Marxist, causes a "metabolic rift" in man's relation with nature (Foster 2002). Capitalism changed the nature of man's relation to nature and alienated him from it (Humphrey 2002). Nature appears to him only as a resource that needs to be exploited. To capitalists, nature is like a pool of capital and they commodify nature. Moreover, capitalism is a system that must continually expand. No growth capitalism is an oxymoron. Capitalism's basic driving force is the amassing of profit and wealth through accumulation process. Because of its expansionist tendencies, it will eventually come up against the reality of finite natural resources. As argued by scholars, in capitalism one can see the conflict between biophysical and social laws. In order to maintain its expansionism capitalism fashions a political judicial and social system to support the system of wealth and accumulation. It promotes fear, greed, competition, individualism, and consumerism and all these characteristics work in conflict with nature.

The importance of an eco-Marxist critique of capitalism lies in the fact that it elevated environmental concerns from the level of moral criticism of industrial revolution to characteristics of capitalism. It provided the clarity that it was not merely industrialization that caused environmental degradation but the relations of capitalism work inherently against nature. Within capitalist system not only the corporates who are engaged in the exploitation of nature, even the individuals, and the state also participate in the process. In capitalism, nobody is free from considering nature as a commodity. Therefore the individual, corporate, and the states contribute their share of destruction. The inequality inherent in capitalism is reflected in the destruction and distribution of environmental issues too. In a way, it was the injustice involved in these systems that generated environmental justice movements. But the process had its implications on the system too.

The movements for sustainable development and environmental justice/ rights had a significant impact on the capitalist production process. Capitalism as a system prefers a minimalist, less interventionist state. It prefers state intervention in the economy only to help manage the crisis of capitalism. The interventionist capitalist state of the welfare model is also considered as a means for managing the crises. But once the market balances in its domain the state withdraw. The welfare capitalist model of the dominant northern democracies underwent important changes since the 1970s. The dominant economies of the North especially the USA and the UK followed the ideals of free market economy under Reagan and Thatcher administrations respectively. It was around the same time that the human rights discourse surrounding environment was marking its presence in the international political arena.

Similarly, most of the western world witnessed strong currents of green movements some of which turned to political parties also. Germany was an important case in context. The growth of International Non-Governmental Organisations committed to the cause of environment and development and political parties with a green agenda created a different political situation for the advocates of free market economy. It is true that a lot of environmental movements, especially in the South, stand against the state as the state form a significant player in the violation of environmental rights. Though a large majority of green movements, parties, and organisations of the world follows an anti-state agenda, many scholars have argued that a close analysis of their programmes and policies in effect demands for a reformed interventionist and democratic state for ensuring environmental protection and rights (Hurrell 1994, Paterson 1999). The pressure politics of the environmental groups led to the incorporation of environmental standards into state policies (Dryzek et.al 2003). In other words, the environmental right discourse provided a space for the state to re-enter the market with environmental rules regulations and standards to protect the environmental rights of the masses. This does not mean that environmental movements were successful in totally affecting the power of the state across the world. The characteristics of the state (state structures) which are as diversified as the green movements were important in this context (Dryzek et.al 2003). That is why some states are greener than others.

The environmental standards instituted due to the pressure from green politics resulted in increased cost of production that stands against the essence of capitalist production i.e profit maximization. Ecological degradation itself can generate a crisis in capitalism. As argued by O' Connor, the impairment of "natural conditions of production" because of environmental degradation can lead to an economic crisis in capitalism viz, underproduction of capital (O' Connor 1998). Though not directly connected to any environmental movement, it was in the year 1988 that the article of James O Connor titled *Capitalism, Nature, Socialism: a Theoretical Introduction* was published, marking the emergence of eco-Marxist critique of capitalism.

Market Laws and Environment: Corporate Environmentalism.

After the incorporation of environmentalism into state's domain and increasing ecological taxation, the advocates of free market produced the idea of free market environmentalism. Free market environmentalism as advocated by Terry Anderson goes against the common notion that market and its expansion as the reason for environmental degradation. Instead, the free market environmentalists argue that applying the market principle can solve the environmental problems. The supporters of free market environmentalism agree with Garrett Hardin's idea of the *tragedy of commons* (1968) i.e un-owned or publicly owned resources will be subjected to exploitation and mismanagement than the privately owned resources (Anderson and Huggins 2008). Therefore they advocated privatization of natural resources. The application of private property rights over natural resources, establishing rewards, incentives, and reduced government regulations are some of the features of free market environmentalism. In Anderson's own words, "free market environmentalism emphasizes the positive incentives associated with prices, profits and entrepreneurship [...] instead of government regulations and taxes".

This does not mean that this model of environmentalism negates the idea of the state. It needs the state to define and regulate the property relations in the environment just like that of any other property relation in the economy. It looks at ways and means to limit political regulations in resolving environmental degradation and tries to harness market forces to improve environmental quality. The increasing environmental awareness, rights discourse and the state intervention through taxation and regulation compelled the corporate to find ways and means to tackle the situation. Corporate environmental practices can be considered as a result of this. Corporate environmentalism which came into the mainstream roughly around the late 1980s or early 1990s refers to the environmental concerns incorporated by corporates in their programme. It refers to the integration of environmental aspects into the planning and execution of a firm's programmes.

Prior to the 1970s environmental aspects seldom found a place in the discussions of marketing strategies. Environmental cost like any other social cost of production and consumption process was considered as an external matter which a corporate was not bothered about. The environment became central to the marketing strategies of the firms only from the late 1980s when environmental movements received a momentum and many environmental laws and regulations were implemented by the state (Menon and Menon 1997). The effort of the firms to incorporate environmental aspects in their decision making and marketing strategy was considered as a way out from increased governmental regulations. These attempts can be considered as the strategy of the corporate in resistance adaptation (Menon and Menon 1997). To Varadarajan and Menon (1988) it was a kind of "mandatory corporate responsibility". The main objective of incorporating environmentalist concerns remains to gain a competitive advantage in the market.

Environmentalism as a Marketing Strategy

Corporate environmentalism can take different dimensions like corporate environmental responsibility, green marketing and the promotion of green consumerism. A significant element of green marketing strategy includes green advertisings and the practices of eco-labeling. The ideological and political intricacies of eco-labeling in co-opting the environmental resistance by the market were subjected to many discussions (see Bostrom and Klintman 2008). The green marketing strategy intends to turn the table to the consumer by promoting the idea of green consumerism.

Green consumerism promotes the consumption of products that are eco-friendly. As a means of shifting the focus from the production process, the corporates promoted the idea of green consumption. Instead of the producer, the consumer obtained the responsibility of protecting nature. The underlying idea was that by consuming responsibly one can save the environment. It was also a kind of extending the market logic of demand and supply to the environmental cause. But the idea of green consumerism puts a blind shields on the very question that how consumers get to control the relations of production in capitalism? Moreover the idea of green does not go well with the practice of consumerism. The terms green and consumerism are incompatible in nature as consumerism always puts the environment in danger. A consumer never reconciles his metabolic relation with nature. Consumerism only promotes the commodification of nature. But the promotion of the idea helps the capitalists to disorient the accusations on the capitalist production relations. The agenda of green consumerism in effect utilizes the environmental consciousness of the consumer in marketing a product. That is why the radical environmentalists have put it aside as a myth (see Smith 1998).

By preying on the fears of ecological crisis or providing a chance to be progressive by being environmentally responsible, the corporates designs green marketing strategies, premier one is their use of ecological or green advertisements. A green advertisement is the one that incorporates environmental aspects to its frame whether or not the product featured is eco-friendly. It is a way of exhibiting the environmental commitment of the firm by incorporating claims of ecological sensitivity.

Based on the ecological claims ecological advertisements can be classified into five categories viz. the claims on the eco-friendliness of the product, the process of production, the commitment of the firm to the ecological cause, ecological fact and a combination of all these claims (Carlson, Grove and Kangun 1993). Major studies in the field of ecological advertisements show that the most common claim in an ecological advertisement is the commitment of the firm towards the cause. But in actuality, most of these advertisements are misleading. They either conceal the real ecological impacts or provides partial information.

The social acceptance of environmentalism and environmental justice is used for advancing the financial interest of the firm. Green advertisements are criticized for *green washing* as it communicates misleading information. By promoting misinformation these advertisements violates many of the consumer rights including the right of the consumer to an informed choice. The analysis of advertisements by critical theorists has explained the ideological role of such advertisements in social reproduction. Information shared by advertisements not only provides a functional explanation of the product but also "social symbolic information" (Leiss, Kline and Jhally 1986). They "inform and mediate social relations" while generating the consciousness on "what to buy for becoming fashionable political progressive, popular successful etc" (Leiss, Kline and Jhally 1986). It deals with a whole lot of status questions. It recreates an ideological environment for the capitalist system in which capitalist consumer culture can deal with an ecological crisis on its own. An example will help in explaining this situation. The Idea Cellular, a mobile network provider in India came up with an ecological advertisement (2010) which encouraged the consumers to rely more on mobile phones for communication. The reason for the recommendation was not the time and space question but was about the deforestation caused by the use of paper for writing letters. The advertisement brings forward the crisis of deforestation but at the same time remain silent about the amount of non-degradable and toxic waste produced by the increased reliance on mobile phones. In a way, it produces a false sense of environmental problems and their solutions. Here it is clear that the aim of the advertisement was developing an eco-friendly face for the company and in doing so it generated misleading information regarding the environmental question of concern.

A study of green advertisements in Indian media proved that 51.7 % of such advertisements were misleading and deceptive in nature (Fernando, Sivakumaran and Suganthi 2014). Even in developed countries, studies show that green advertisements were nothing more than green corporate image building exercises (Banerjee, Gulas and Iyer 1995, Baum 2012). The green marketing strategies whether it is eco-labeling or green advertisements tend to conceal the ecological damage involved in the capitalist production and consumption process. It gives the impression that by consuming the particular product the consumer is participating in her share of environmental movement or indirectly contributing to environmental protection.

Conclusion

In course of time, environment achieved its status as a prominent theme of human rights discourse. Subsequently, the state intervention for the environment in the economy was legitimized. It ensured many environmental regulations at the initiative of the state. The enactment of environmental laws and regulations compelled the advocates of the free market in envisioning a new strategy to adapt to the context. The capability of the capitalist system lies in its successful appropriation of the human right debate surrounding environment by envisioning green marketing strategies. In fact, the corporates under the compulsion or the necessity of following environmental regulations established subsidiaries specializing in the environment. It became a part of the business expansion of capitalist firms. Environmental expertise in the contemporary political economy is a profitable subsector of many corporates. Therefore like many other rights born with capitalism in the period of industrial revolution, this new right which emerged as a direct opposite of industrial development also became an instrument for capital to maintain its hold and expand its power. The autonomy of environmentalism from the political economy of capitalism is becoming very limited and struggling for survival.

References

Anderson, L Terry and Laura E Huggins (2008) *Greener than Thou: Are You Really an Environmentalist?*, Hoover Institution press: Stanford.

Banerjee, S. C S Gulas and E Iyaer (1995) "Shades of Green: a Multi Dimensional Analysis of Environmental Advertising", Journal of Advertising, 24:2, 21-31.

Baum, Lauren M (2012) "It's not Easy Being Green...or Is It? A Content Analysis of Environmental Claims in Magazine Advertisements from USA and UK", Environmental Communication, 6:4, 423-40.

Bostrom, Magnus and Mikael Klintman (2008) Eco-standards Product Labeling and Green Consumerism, Palgrave Macmillan: UK.

Carlson, Les. Stephen J Grove and Norman Kangun (1993) "A Content Analysis of Environmental Advertising Claims: A Matrix method Approach", Journal of Advertising, 22:3, 27-39.

Dobson, Andrew. (1998) Justice and Environment: Conceptions of Environmental Sustainability and Dimensions of Social Justice, OUP: Oxford.

Drysek, John S. et.al (2003) Green States and Social Movements: Environmentalism in the Unites States, United Kingdom, Germany and Norway, OUP: Oxford.

Fernando, Angeline Gautami, Bharadhwaj Sivakumarn and L Suganthi (2014) "Nature of Green Advertisements in India: are they Green Washed?" Asian Journal of Communication, 24:3, 222-41.

Foster, J B (2000) Marx's Ecology Materialism and Nature, Monthly Review press: New York.

Foster, J B (2002) "Capitalism and Ecology: the Nature of Contradiction", Monthly Review Press, 54:4. https://monthlyreview.org/2002/09/01/capitalism-and-ecology/ Accessed on 01-11-2017.

Guha, Ramachandra (2000) Environmentalism a Global History, OUP: New Delhi.

Humphrey, Mathew (2002) *Preservation versus the People: Nature Humanity* and Political Philosophy, OUP: Oxford.

Hurrell, Andrew (1994) "A Crisis of Ecological Viability: Global Environmental Change and the Nation States" Political Studies, XLII, 146-165.

Idea Cellular (Advertisement) Idea paper Save advertisement, Chrome picture Private Limited January 2010. https://www.youtube.com/watch?v=bBuAUKJXZGw accessed on 02-11-2017.

Leiss, William. Stephen Kline and Sut Jhally (1986) Social Communication in Advertising: Persons Products and Images of Wellbeing, Metheuen: New York.

Menon, Ajay and Anil Menon (1997) "Enviropreneurial Market Strategy: the Emergence of Corporate Environmentalism as a Marketing Strategy", Journal of Marketing, 61:1, 51-67.

O'Connor, James. (1998) Natural Causes: essays in Ecological Marxism, Guilford Press: New York.

Paterson, Matthew (1999) "Green Political Strategy and the State" in N Ben Fairweather et.al (eds) Environmental Futures, Macmillan: London, 73-102.

Smith, M Toby (1998) The Myth of Green Marketing: Tending our Goats at the Edge of Apocalypse, University of Toronto Press: London.

UN General Assembly (1972) Declaration of the United Nations Conference on Human Environment. December 1972, Stockholm.

Varadarajan, P Rajan and Anil Menon (1988) "Cause Related Marketing: a Co-alignment of Marketing Strategy and Corporate Philanthropy" Journal of Marketing, 52:6, 58-74.

7

Environmental Governance and Human Rights in India

—*Anju Lis Kurian and C. Vinodan*

Introduction

Environmental governance is the processes and institutions through which societies make decisions that affect the environment. It is a specific form of the wider term 'governance'. In addition environmental governance is primarily about how to reach environmental goals and can be measured by the effectiveness of strategies as well as initiatives implemented to achieve environmental goals. Good environmental governance needs the participation of stakeholders, access to information, adequate funding, transparency, accountability etc. Organisations, policy instruments, financing mechanisms, rules, procedures and norms which regulate the process of global environmental protection are involved in the global environmental governance (Wingqvist et al. 2012: 14-15). Thus, the term environmental governance can be defined as: 'the ability of a state to govern its resources as prescribed in forms of legal instruments and supplemented by policy, programme and institutional interventions, all operating in a holistic manner with effective synergies among and within the various entities, taking into consideration the social, cultural, environmental and economic factors (Singh 2014: 604).' On the other hand, human rights are the basic rights and freedoms entitled to all human beings, as reflected in the Universal Declaration on Human Rights, in Principle 1 of the Stockholm Declaration, in the Millennium Development Goals, and in the Universal Declaration on the Rights of Indigenous Peoples. Human rights include civil and political rights, such as the rights to life, liberty and freedom of expression, to worship, to own property, and to be treated equally before the law. They also comprise economic, social and cultural rights, such as the rights to family, to education, to culture, to health, to subsistence, to residence and movement, and to inviolability of the home. These rights are universal and fundamental, and states have the obligation to guarantee these rights (Kurian and Vinodan 2016: 431).

Usually, environmental governance is shaped by a collection of Multilateral Environmental Agreements (MEAs), political agreements, non-binding agreements, programmes, projects and national laws enacted at various occasions. Numerous policies regarding environment are executed at the international level while others are done at the regional and national levels which are endorsed by a copious of stakeholders and a multitude of implementing agencies (Singh 2014: 601). Multilateral Environmental Agreements offer the global framework for governance in regions and countries. The present structure of environmental governance is developed out of the United Nations Conference on the Human Environment at Stockholm, Sweden in 1972, the United Nations Conference on Environment and Development at Rio de Janeiro, Brazil in 1992, and the World Summit on Sustainable Development at Johannesburg, South Africa in 2002. The three basic elements evolved from the decades of global efforts for environmental governance are the following (1) First element is that a collection of intergovernmental organizations such as the United Nations Environmental Programme (UNEP), the United Nations Development Programme (UNDP) and other specialized agencies and commissions that are responsible for co-ordinating policy on the environment at the international level; (2) secondly, it is the framework of international environmental law that has developed over several decades, such as the Rotterdam Convention on Prior Informed Consent (PIC) and Stockholm Convention on Persistent Organic Pollutants (POPs); and (3) thirdly, it is the financing mechanisms such as the Global Environmental Facility (GEF) that supports capacity building to carry out treaty commitments, supplements national efforts towards sustainable development in poorer countries and UN agencies and treaty secretariats that co-ordinate and carry out environmental efforts. All these three elements together set priorities and facilitate steps to protect the environment at different levels (Fakier et. al. 2005: 13).

At the same time the series of international agreements has increased the understanding that biodiversity conservation necessitates the participation of the rural communities who live in natural ecosystems. This perspective has also reflected in the Indian national policy processes and pronouncements which have emphasized the need for widespread conservation efforts by including the interests of local communities (Kurian 2016a). By and large governments are the central actors in the governance, management, exploitation and conservation of environment. But now-a-days actors outside the government are equally play a vital role because meaningful participation of all sectors of society became a crucial element in effective environmental governance. The failure in taking consideration of public opinion and their involvement can lead to conflict and resistance. On the other hand participation and inputs from public provides a voice to society and legitimacy to decision-making processes. The Principle 10 of Rio Declaration 1992 enunciated public access to information, participation in decision making, and access to justice as main doctrines of environmental governance. Again a decade later, in 2002 one hundred governments reiterated the importance of these goals (Fakier et. al. and 2005: 4, 16 & 19). In several countries specific areas are notified as Protected Areas (PAs) for wildlife conservation as a way of reducing pressures on wildlife as well as biodiversity (Lasgorceix and Kothari 2009: 37).

Today more than five percent of India's land surface managed under the Protected Area regime. The Protected Areas in India are categorized as National Parks, Tiger Reserves, Wild life Sanctuaries etc. It is estimated that there are three to four million inhabitants are there in these PAs and several million more living in adjacent or nearby areas, whose livelihoods depend on natural resources from these PAs. The local communities traditionally have unclear or unregistered right to natural resources as well as lands. Even though human habitation and uses of natural resources are forbidden or strictly controlled within most PAs. The circumstances of local communities within PAs are very pathetic. They are living in a state of deprivation, poverty and in conflict with PA managers, who usually perceive them as being responsible for the loss of wildlife. They have unreliable access to natural resources for survival and livelihoods and many development facilities like access to basic amenities, transport, health and education facilities and land development do not reach adequately to them. In addition man-animal conflict is prevalent in these areas through crop and livestock damage, human injury or death and retaliatory killings of animals (Lasgorceix and Kothari 2009: 37). The process of park creation also imposes further restrictions on the survival and development activities of the indigenous as well as lowincome villagers. Within the newly created protected areas development and infrastructure activities are not permitted besides strict restrictions on the harvest of forest products which are significant constituent of their traditional livelihood (Ghate and Ghate 2011: 6). Therefore, it is essential that conservation must be discussed within the context of human rights or in other words human rights approaches should incorporate the necessity of conserving natural ecosystems and resources. In the milieu of PAs, conservation strategies must deal with the concern of ensuring livelihood security and freedom from poverty as well as impoverishment (Wani and Kothari 2007: 102).

Environmental Governance and Human Rights

Approximately 70 percent of the Indian population depends on land-based occupations, forests, wet-lands and marine habitats for their fundamental subsistence requisites. This reliance is prevalent across the country with an exemption to very few 'natural' ecosystems in some inaccessible reaches of the Himalayas and in some islands that are not being subjected to some form of human touch. They look upon the resources of the area to satisfy their basic needs such as water, housing material, fuel wood, fodder, pastures, medicinal plants, non-timber forest products (NTFP), timber, aquatic resources including fish, spiritual and cultural sustenance and myriad other livelihood purposes (Wani and Kothari 2007: 101). The utmost inconsistency regarding the right to use natural resources for livelihood purposes exist in PAs. The subcontinent of India is the best example of the tensions between conservation and human development (Ghate and Ghate 2011: 6). The reason is that protected Areas are intended exclusively for biodiversity conservation and extremely preservationist in character. Along with this PAs systems are governed by horribly strict management regimes with local communities having little role in utilization, management and conservation (Gadgil et. al. 2011: 178). This approach has led to several difficulties including human rights violations of the local communities.

Over the last few decades, several hundred PAs have been declared under the Wild Life Protection Act (WLPA) of 1972. Presently by including such areas prior to 1972 which were declared under previous laws, mostly colonial in origin country has over 600 PAs. Until 2003 PAs are mainly belonged to two categories: National Parks where all human activities are strictly prohibited and Wildlife Sanctuaries where some activities or rights are allowed. Then Conservation Reserves and Community Reserves are the two more categories of PAs added to the list. Again there are a number of other legal and non-legal categories of PAs contributing diverse degrees of conservation coverage to specific sites namely protected and reserved forests (under the Indian Forest Act 1927), biosphere reserves, elephant reserves, heritage sites (none of these with legal backing), tiger reserves (declared since 1973 but given legal backing only in 2006), and ecologically sensitive areas (under the Environment Protection Act 1986). The WLPA has a significant role in decreasing the devastation of wildlife species and habitats, but it sustained the colonial legacy of rendering management of natural resources into the hands of centralized bureaucracies by taking away the remaining influence on governance and control that rests with local communities. This has directly or indirectly affected the life of 3 to 4 million people in indigenous and other communities living in PAs and another millions of inhabitants surrounding PAs who depend on PAs for their livelihoods. A nationwide assessment conducted in the mid-1980s demonstrates that 69 percent of the studied PAs had human populations (Wani and Kothari 2007:102-103).

Most of the protected areas around the world fall under six different IUCN categories corresponding to specific management objectives that allow ever-increasing human use, from category 1 (strict reserve) to category 6 (managed resource use). It is noteworthy that the actual presence and influence of human beings in a given protected area depends on the extent to which management objectives and laws assigned to that category are put into effect (Agrawal and Redford 2009: 4). The most apparent solution for tackling the problems of people within protected areas is to relocate them outside the protected area. In many instances the use of force was critical to displacement from protected areas such displacements have caused impoverishment, social disarticulation, political disempowerment etc. The long-recognized and worst impacts of the creation of protected areas are the adverse effects on the incomes of those who are displaced, even if they live within or in the vicinity of newly formed protected areas. Several studies have recognized the significant direct losses to livelihoods and agricultural incomes, human-wildlife interactions, and indirect losses due to the loss of access to areas set aside for conservation (Agrawal and Redford 2009: 5).

The two major assumptions relevant in the context of displacement is that human presence has a negative impact on conservation, and that there is a calculus of gains and losses through which the worst effects of involuntary displacement on humans can be balanced by gains of conservation through displacement (Agrawal and Redford 2009: 5). In addition, the renascent 'protection ideology' in international biodiversity conservation articulates that current Integrated Conservation and Development Projects (ICDPs) or people-oriented approaches to the governance of protected areas are failing. The supporters of this 'protection ideology' are adamant that the presence of people in protected areas is anathema to their ideas. Based on this 'protection ideology' a large number of protected area managers are firm on the belief that human displacement is indispensible for conservation. On the one side protected areas have done much good in terms of biodiversity conservation on the other side the increase in protected areas led to an increase in the number of people displaced to create the space for protected areas. These displaced people to make room for protected areas are known as 'conservation refugees' (Awuh 2011: 2). Conservation refugees are people displaced by the creation of protected areas are actually the victims of ecological expropriation. They are forced to move into the subsistence landscapes, migrating to informal sectors of towns and villages with no customary land titles, and end up in wage-labour ranks if they manage to find any work at all. More than that prohibiting access to indigenous and other people in parks and protected areas is 'involuntary displacement' even when physical displacement and relocation are not required (Awuh 2011: 3). There cannot make a comparison between conservation refugees ecological or environmental refugees. Environmental refugees are people forced to abandon their homelands as a result of adverse conditions such as unbearable heat or cold, famine, flooding, disease, desertification, drought and other consequences of climate chaos. Other refugees can go across national boundaries and gather in rehabilitation centres but conservation refugees have few logical gathering points and are difficult to spell out their number (Dowie 2006).

In India, according to a recent review the number of people displaced from protected areas from the 1970s up to 2008 is approximately 100,000. Further displacements of similar scale are planned and going on in this decade (2010–20) also with the aim of consolidating and expanding the protected area system (Shahabuddin and Bhamidipati 2014: 122). This has adversely affected millions of people whose livelihoods depend upon non-timber forest products (NTFP), which contributes 14 percent to 23 percent of the rural income for economically weak communities who are marginalized in the society (Kanagavel et al. 2013: 61). Moreover, in many places the restoration of ecosystems has enhanced wildlife populations with spilling out phenomenon and intermittent crop raids, threats to livestock or even to human life. The incident of man-animal conflict is relatively new but it is greater than ever where livelihood and conservation agendas are competing for survival as well as existence. The continued increase in human-wildlife conflicts is a topic of grave concern with multitudinous reverberations across the society. Communities have been looking for aid to resolve these conflicts, which in some places are weakening the resolve to continue conservation efforts (Kothari and Pathak 2010: 187). The fast moving efforts of the Indian government to relocate villages are likely as a response to the findings that endangered animal species such as the Bengal tiger are dilapidated due to poaching, forest degradation, and habitat fragmentation. The issue of conservation-induced displacement incites acute reactions from conservationists due to widely varying opinions both of its conservation need as well as its socio-economic impacts (Shahabuddin and Bhamidipati 2014: 122).

Exclusionary approaches to protected area governance are usually associated with human-rights violations beyond the underlying land-rights infringements, as local people are subjected to evictions, harassment, and conflicts with park law-enforcement personnel over access to their critical resources. The absence of legal recognition and allied recourse mechanisms also constrains the ability of local people to join in fighting broader governance failures such as allocation of mining and other extractive activities in these regions (Springer and Almeida 2015: 21). In most of the time conservation organizations are much concerned about the protection of flora and fauna than the well-being of the area's inhabitants. Therefore, the objective of double sustainability cannot be attained and that will affect the relationship between local people and protected areas in a negative way. The consensus from the experiences across the world is that protected areas operate much more effectively as well as successfully when they are managed with or by inhabitants themselves (Awuh 2011: x).

From the 2003 Durban World Parks Congress came out a 'new paradigm' which reflected an increasing appreciation of the significant roles of Indigenous Peoples and local communities in conservation of the Earth's biodiversity and the importance of fully incorporating their rights and interests in protected areas.

However, mechanisms to promote and ensure adherence to human rights principles and standards in environmental governance lag a significant gap (Springer and Almeida 2015: 29). The Durban Congress put forward a set of good governance principles for protected areas which are the following: 1) 'legitimacy and voice' that means ensuring the capacity of men and women to influence decisions, on the basis of freedom of association and speech), 2) 'subsidiarity' with the intension of attributing management authority and responsibility to the institutions closest to the resources at stake, 3) 'fairness' in sharing equitably the costs and benefits of conservation and providing recourse to impartial judgment in case of conflict, 4) 'doing no harm' i.e. making sure that the costs of conservation are not dumped on some weak social actors without any form of compensation, 5) 'direction' in 'establishing long-term conservation objectives grounded in an appreciation of ecological, historical, social and cultural complexities', 6) 'performance' means meeting the needs and concerns of all stakeholders while making a wise use of resources, and 7) 'accountability' for having clearly demarcated lines of responsibility and ensuring a transparent flow of information about processes and institutions. However, the above principles are important overarching them all is the respect for human rights. Thus, a rights-based approach is viewed as the most justified means of conservation. Today the International Union for Conservation of Nature (IUCN) also has the same perspective in its environmental governance approach (Borrini-Feyerabend et al. 2004).

At anytime anywhere stakeholders' access to information, adequate funding, transparency and accountability are essential aspects of apposite environmental governance (Wingqvist et al. 2012: 14-15). Conservation activities that involve the displacement of communities and denial of allied livelihood of the inhabitants have local as well as global impact. Denunciation of free and prior informed approval by indigenous peoples and other local communities will again intensify these impacts, with respect to their rights, lands and territories. So it should be take into account that the human rights aspects of such eviction process need to be cautiously measured in designing these policies and projects irrespective of geographic region (CIEL 2011: 9). There is an extraordinary dearth of good information about the social impacts of protected areas. Most of the existing literature merely mentioned conservation displacement or evictions, with none of the details regarding social discontent, livelihood issues and human rights violations of affected population (Kurian 2016a). A plethora of world's affluent biodiversity spots are found in the tropics which also include populations suffering rigorous economic disadvantages that are about 60 percent of the world's poorest people. In these regions an approximately 75 percent of the populations live below the poverty line of US$ 1 per day. Accomplishment of conservation in such areas is not sustainable if it again aggravates the marginalization and impoverishment of the local population and ignores their development requirements (Awuh 2011: 71).

The remarkable achievements from protected areas in the last generation have however been accompanied by silence over its socio-economic expenses to conservation refugees. In a nutshell evictions without provision for superior livelihoods will be a source of misery to local people displaced for conservation. Till date there is no universally acceptable methodology for estimating the number of people displaced from protected areas globally. Research inputs from the fields of anthropology, conservation biology, ethnobiology and ethnoecology have corroborated that the world's biodiversity will only be effectively conserved by preserving diversity of culture and vice versa (Kurian 2016b). The protected areas that are surrounded by angry and hungry people who describe themselves as 'enemies of conservation' are generally doomed to fail (Dowie 2006). The experiences show that a bottom-top approach has proved to be really effective in conservation instances around the globe. This bottom-top gives local people a sense of responsibility and increases community participation as opposed to the top-bottom approach which makes local people feel excluded from the conservation efforts. Conservation projects which exclude local people may conserve natural resources to an extent but not conserve human resources that mean peoples' access to livelihood. In order to achieve double sustainability in conservation it is wise to involve local people in environmental governance (Awuh 2011: 176).

Conclusion

In the 21st century environmental governance has become one of the foremost concerns of international community particularly in the scenario of global climate change. In most of the landscapes of India wildlife and people live side by side where people- exclusive conservation raises severe human rights challenges. So the equity of human rights and biodiversity conservation needs more attention by government and scholars as it also has direct implications for the success of environmental governance across the country. People inclusive conservation efforts and bottom –top approach is the only preferable solution to tackle the issues of human rights violations in connection with environmental governance. The sooner India moves in this direction, the better it will be for both its wildlife and its people. It is the only path that has a long-term hope of success in India by being the second largest populated country of the world.

Reference

Shahabuddin, Ghazala and Bhamidipati, Padmasai (2014): "Conservation-induced Displacement: Recent Perspectives from India", *Environmental Justice*, 7(5): 122-129.

Springer, Jenny and Almeida, Fernanda (2015): *Protected Areas and the Land Rights of Indigenous Peoples and Local Communities: Current Issues and Future Agenda*, Report of Rights and Resources Initiative.

Wani, Milind and Kothari, Ashish (2007): "Protected areas and human rights in India—the impact of the official conservation model on local communities", *Policy Matters*, 15: 100-114.

Borrini-Feyerabend,, Grazia, Kothari, Ashish and Oviedo, Gonzalo (2004): *Indigenous and Local Communities and Protected Areas: Towards Equity and Enhanced Conservation*, Cambridge : Gland.

Lasgorceix, Antoine and Kothari, Ashish (2009): "Displacement and Relocation of Protected Areas: A Synthesis and Analysis of Case Studies", *Economic & Political Weekly*, XLIV (49): 37-47.

Fakier, Saliem, Stephens, Anthea, Tholin, Jenny and Kapelus, Paul (2005): *Environmental Governance*, Background Research Paper produced for the South Africa Environment Outlook report on behalf of the Department of Environmental Affairs and Tourism.

Kurian, Anju Lis (2016a): *Climate change and environmental governance: The role of international funding*, National seminar on biodiversity of microbes & climate change mitigation, organized by The Research & Post Graduate Department of Botany, Catholicate College Pathanamthitta.

Kurian, Anju Lis (2016b): "Climate change & Environmental protection in South Asia: The making of conservation refugees", International seminar on Environmental Security & Sustainable Development (October 19-21), organized by UNESCO Madanjeet Singh Institute of South Asia Regional Cooperation & Center for South Asian Studies, Pondicherry University, Pondicherry.

Kurian, Anju Lis and Vinodan, C. (2016): 'Environmental conservation & human rights issues: The case of Western Ghats in India', in C. Subramanian and M. Sugirtha (Eds.), *Human Rights in India: Current Issues and Challenges*, Konganadu Publications: Tamil Nadu.

Wingqvist, Gunilla Olund, Olof Drakenberg, Daniel Slunge, Martin Sjostedt and Anders Ekbom (2012): *The Role of Governance for Improved Environmental Outcomes: Perspectives for Developing Countries and Countries in Transition*, Sweden: The Swedish Environmental Protection Agency.

Singh, Asha (2014): *Environmental Governance in Small Island Developing States*, United Nations Environment Programme (UNEP), Nairobi, Kenya.

Ghate, Rucha and Ghate, Suresh (2011): *A story of conservation refugees: vulnerability and coping strategies*, Paper presented at ICARUS-2 conference, University of Michigan, 5-8th May.

Gadgil, Madhav, R. J. Ranjit Daniels, K. N. Ganeshaiah, S. Narendra Prasad, M. S. R. Murthy, C. S. Jha, B. R. Ramesh and K. A. Subramanian (2011): "Mapping Ecologically Sensitive, Significant and Salient Areas of Western Ghats: Proposed Protocols And Methodology", *Current Science*, 100(2): 175-182.

Agrawal, Arun and Redford, Kent (2009): Conservation and Displacement: An Overview, *Conservation and Society*, 7(1): 1-10.

Awuh, Harrison Esam (2011): *A Critique of the Global Literature on the Conservation Refugee Problem*, A thesis in fulfillment of the requirements for the degree of Master of Science in Geography, Submitted to Victoria University of Wellington.

Dowie, Mark (2006): "Conservation refugees: When protecting nature means kicking people out", *Seedling*, January: 6-12.

Kanagavel, Arun, Shijo Joseph, Revati Pandya and Rajeev Raghavan (2013): "Potential for Community and Conservation Reserves in the Western Ghats, India", *Asian Journal of Conservation Biology*, 2(1): 61-68.

Kothari, Ashish and Pathak, Neema (2010): 'Indigenous and Local Community Based Conservation in India: Current Status and Future Prospects', in Kristen Walker Painemilla, Anthony B. Rylands, Alisa Woofter and Cassie Hughes (Eds.), *Indigenous Peoples and Conservation: From Rights to Resource Management*, Arlington, VA: Conservation International.

CIEL (2011): *Climate Change & Human Rights: A Primer*, The Center for International Environmental Law, Geneva, www.ciel.org.

8

Right to Water and Women: Privatisation, Equity and Gender

— Devi Parvathy

The 1992 Dublin Principles, the Kyoto Declaration in 2003 accompanied by the 2010 United Nations General Assembly resolution recognizing the human right to water and the Millennium Development Goals (MDGs) have created a new notion as to how water should be treated as a common good regardless of hierarchies and gender. For the first time in history the right to water has been placed on a higher pedestal inviting applause from international water groups, advocates and people affected by water problems.

The Dublin Statement on Water and Sustainable Development, also known as the Dublin Principles, was a meeting of experts on water related problems that took place on 31 January 1992 at the International Conference on Water and the Environment (ICWE), Dublin, Ireland. Five hundred participants, including government- designated experts from a hundred countries and representatives of eighty international, intergovernmental, and nongovernmental, organizations attended the Conference. The Guiding Principles of the Dublin Statement on Water and Sustainable Development are as follows:

1. Fresh water is finite and vulnerable resource, essential to sustain life, development and the environment.
2. Water development and management should be based on a participatory approach, involving users, planners and policy-makers at all levels.
3. Women play a central part in the provision, management and safeguarding of water.

4. Water has an economic value in all its competing uses and should be recognized as an economic good, (Staddon, Appleby, and Grant 2012: 67).

On 28 July 2010, through Resolution 64/292, the United Nations General Assembly explicitly recognized the human right to water and sanitation and acknowledged that clean drinking water and sanitation are essential to the realisation of all human rights. The Resolution calls upon States and international organisations to provide financial resources for capacity-building and technology transfer to help countries, in particular developing countries, to provide safe, clean, accessible and affordable drinking water and sanitation for all. The human right to water is indispensable for leading a life in human dignity. It is a prerequisite for the realization of other human rights. Right to water is defined as the right of everyone to sufficient, safe, acceptable and physically accessible and affordable water for personal and domestic uses. The target of *Millennium Development Goal 7* calls to "halve, by 2015, the proportion of the population without sustainable access to safe drinking water and basic sanitation".

The human right to water and sanitation entitles "everyone to sufficient, safe, acceptable, physically accessible and affordable water for personal and domestic uses." (United Nations, 2002). Each component needs further elaboration.

Sufficiency The water supply for each person must be sufficient and for continuous personal and domestic uses. These uses ordinarily include drinking, personal sanitation, washing of clothes, food preparation, personal and household hygiene. According to the World Health Organization (WHO), between 50 and 100 litres of water per person per day are needed to ensure that most basic needs are met and few health concerns arise.

Safety The water required for each personal or domestic use must be safe, therefore free from micro-organisms, chemical substances and radiological hazards that constitute a threat to a person's health. Measures of drinking-water safety are usually defined by national and/or local standards for drinking-water quality. The *World Health Organization (WHO) Guidelines for Drinking-Water Quality* provides a basis for the development of national standards that, if properly implemented, will ensure the safety of drinking-water.

Acceptability Water should be of an acceptable colour, odour and taste for each personal or domestic use. [...] All water facilities and services must be *culturally* appropriate and sensitive to gender, lifecycle and privacy requirements.

Physically accessibility Everyone has the right to a water and sanitation service that is physically accessible within, or in the immediate vicinity of the household, educational institution, workplace or health institution. According to WHO, the water source has to be within 1,000 metres of the home and collection time should not exceed 30 minutes.

Affordability Water, and water facilities and services, must be affordable for all. The United Nations Development Programme (UNDP) suggests that water costs should not exceed 3 per cent of household income.

The right to water imposes three types of obligations on State Parties:

- Respect. Governments must refrain from unfairly interfering with people's access to water, for example, by disconnecting their water supply.
- Protect. Governments must protect people's access to water from interference by others, for example, by preventing pollution.
- Fulfill. Governments must adopt the necessary measures directed towards full realisation of the right, for example, by passing legislation, devising and implementing programmes, allocating budgets and monitoring their progress.

The Human Rights to Water focuses on the amount of water necessary for basic human needs (about 50 litres per person per day), which is a small amount in comparison to the large quantities used for economic development (1500 litres per person per day in France). The right to drinking water does not broach general issues linked to environmental protection or integrated management of resources. The right to water has been explicitly recognised in a number of legally binding treaties. The right to water is also an integral part of other human rights, such as the right to life, which is contained in the International Covenant on Civil and Political Rights (1966), and the rights to health, food, housing and an adequate standard of living, which are included in the International Covenant on Economic Social and Cultural Rights (1966). These rights are also provided for in a series of other international and regional treaties.

Privatisation of Water

During the Third World Water Forum in March 2003, the private sector received the global consensus that it was best suited for managing the world's water systems of the South. Water as a human right had not been acknowledged or addressed yet, so global financial entities like the World Bank used the Kyoto forum to address its agenda on water financing. Specifically, the big water companies were concerned about their ability to be sustainable without any financial guarantees from the international financial institutions. The Kyoto Declaration embodied the philosophy that in the development sector came to be known as liberal environmentalism, green neoliberalism, or market environmentalism; all of which are considered a, "mode of resource regulation which aims to deploy markets as the solution to environmental problems," (Bakker 2012). While the idea of water as a human right was not at all mentioned in the declarations in Kyoto, many water industry members began to associate and favor the idea of water as a human right, and so private corporations argued that the best way to fulfill the human right to water was allowing private water corporations the ability to market, properly regulate, and dispense water, (Bakker 2012).

The different functions and values of water can be divided in three complementary levels:

- *Water for life* concerns providing water for the survival of both human beings (individual and collective) and other living beings. This must be recognized as the highest priority in order to guarantee the sustainability of ecosystems so that access for all to a minimum quantity of good quality water is recognised as one of the human rights.
- *Water for citizens* concerns providing water for general interest purposes, as regards public health or the promotion of values of equity or social cohesion, must be ranked at the second level of priority, in connection with citizen's social rights and in the general interest of society as a whole. This is the role of public institutions.
- *Water for development* is an economic function relating to production activities which in general concerns private interests like irrigation for agriculture, hydroelectricity, or industry. This function consumes the largest part of all water resources from rivers and aquifers, and is, therefore, largely responsible for the problems of scarcity and pollution arising in the world. This production-based demand must be managed in accordance with economic efficiency, social equity and environmental sustainability and should occupy the third level of priority. The 'right to water'

should be distinguished from 'water rights' which generally refers to accessing or using water for specific purposes. Law concerning water rights may define who can use water and under which circumstances. Individuals can be allocated water rights which may consist of a predefined amount of water for specific purposes under specific conditions (e.g. farmers have water rights for irrigation purposes). However, these two types of right are interlinked.

Water for development clearly states the drive towards commoditization and privatization of water. For the sake of development nature (natural resources) must be shrunk. The demand for water for domestic, irrigation as well as commercial purposes is growing everyday more so in the developing world due to faster rate of growth of the population, increasing number of people migrating to the cities where fresh water is limited, increase in the per capita consumption of water, increasing consumption by industry (e.g. soft drinks, manufacturing of cars and computers), irrigation of crops particularly meant for export that require more water, pollution of surface water, deforestation, and introduction of pesticides and chemical fertilisers in water (WIDE 2004). The state has failed to cope with the growing demand for water, which is proffered as a reason to open avenues for the private sector to participate in the process of providing the service.

Privatization of water is a process of expansion of the market that creates new property relations and in so doing generates new society-nature relations. Further, it allows private foreign entities the control of other and usually, poor and/or developing nations' water through its regulation, pricing and management. There have seen a considerable growth in the neoliberalization of nature, with its most drastic shifts occurring in the realm of water governance (Harris 2009; Goldman 2007). Particularly in the developing world, rapid urbanization and population growth have put city water systems under great institutional and financial pressure. Global financial institutions such as the International Monetary Fund, the World Bank, and the Asian Development Bank have loaned money to these hard–pressed cities, promoting a neoliberal shift which has included devolution of water management to communities and an increased commoditization of water sector and rapid privatization of water service provision (Bakker 2005; Goldman 2007). As a result, in 2000, governments of 93 nations had begun to privatize their drinking water and wastewater services.

Privatisation has made intrusions to management of natural resources in the last decade and a half, particularly with expanding extraction, reorganising of the production systems to cater to the export markets (Kothari and Ahmad 2003). The livelihoods of a vast majority of rural populations are directly dependent on natural resources – land, water and forests. What is observed is that privatisation is a threat to the farmers, particularly the small and marginal sections. Poor women in particular are the worst affected as they are the non-asset owners and providers of the critical household resources such as water, food, fodder and fuel. Ng (2000:6) opines that under the guise of free market restructuring, the privatisation of public services has led not only to its reduced availability, but also to higher pricing of such services as well as basic necessities for survival. As women are caretakers of families and home-makers, they have to bear the disproportionate burden of providing for the household resources against increasing costs of public utilities, including water.

Privatization of water is a process of expansion of the market that creates new property relations and in so doing generates new society-nature relations. Further, it allows private foreign entities the control of other and usually, poor and/or developing nations' water through its regulation, pricing and management (Bakker 2010). Privatisation of water does not seem to be different from the pattern of privatisation in other service sectors. Evidences from different parts of the world show no commitment to expand access to low income consumers, inequity in the quality of services based on ability to pay, service cut offs, weak regulatory oversight, and lack of accountability to local consumer needs (Grusky 2002). The only difference between water and other market commodities is that the in-take of water cannot be reduced or restricted or depend on people's affordability as human body requires a certain amount of water for survival. Petrella (2001) argues that there is a peculiar irrationality and un-justifiability of commodification and privatisation of water and that is the reason why it took longer for it to follow the trend of other goods. With the advent of privatisation, the state monopoly over water is getting transformed to corporate monopoly through various modes. The different forms of privatisation are – (a) complete sale of public water systems and water treatment plants like in Great Britain; (b) the most common form referred to as PPP (public-private partnerships), where the governments award concessions or leases to water corporations, who then deliver the services and assume costs for operation and maintenance of the system; (c) a more restricted model, in which a corporation is contracted by the government to manage water services for an administrative fee (Barlow and Clarke 2003), and as compensation a charge is levied and there is of course a clear profit motive.

Water equity

Water equity has social, economic, spatial and temporal dimensions. Depending on the scale of analysis distribution of water can vary between sectors of an economy (e.g., industry versus agriculture), countries on a river, upstream-downstream communities along a water course, households reliant on a common water source. Socially we can understand water equity in terms of differences in access and use between men and women, ethnic majorities and minorities, indigenous and non-indigenous, rich and poor, livelihoods, rural and urban people, present and future generations

Though many water resource development interventions have been premised on increasing the supply of water to people and for food, there are rising disparities between the rich and poor within and between countries regarding access to water. Despite there being sufficient freshwater for all people's basic needs one in five people globally are without access to clean water, and close to two and a half billion people lack access to safe sanitation. By 2025 it is estimated that, without a radical shift in policy and re-allocation of resources, some two thirds of the world's population will experience some form of water stress.

Inequitable access to water disproportionately affects the poorest in communities, indicating socio-economic and political processes play an important role in influencing water access. Moreover, this inequality is gendered in its impacts, as women and girls in most societies bear the primary responsibility of water collection and caring for the ill. The urban poor, particularly those in marginalised areas or slums, are usually reliant on insecure, unclean water supplies, which are often provided by private entrepreneurs at expensive rates. It is well documented that the poor in these circumstances often pay more for their water than those who are more well-off (Gutierrez et al., 2003; UNESCO 2003).

According to (UNDP, 2006; UNESCO, 2009; WHO, 2010; UN-HABITAT, 2007)

- Around the world more than 2.6 billion people—over 40 per cent of the world's population—do not have basic sanitation, and
- Most of the people categorized as lacking access to clean water use about 5 litres a day-one tenth of the average daily amount used in rich countries to flush toilets.
- More than one billion people still use unsafe sources of drinking water.

- Four out of every ten people in the world don't have access even to a simple latrine.
- Five million people, mostly children, die each year from water-borne diseases.
- Average water use ranges from 200-300 litres a person a day in most countries in Europe to less than 10 litres in countries such as Mozambique. People lacking access to improved water in developing countries consume far less, partly because they have to carry it over long distances and water is heavy. For the 884 million people or so people in the world who live more than 1 kilometre from a water source, water use is often less than 5 litres a day of unsafe water.
- In Tajikistan nearly a third of the population takes water from canals and irrigation ditches, with risks of exposure to polluted agricultural run-off.
- People living in the slums of Jakarta, Manila and Nairobi pay 5 to 10 times more for water than those living in high-income areas in those same cities and more than consumers in London or New York. In Manila, the cost of connecting to the utility represents about three months' income for the poorest 20% of households, rising to six months' in urban Kenya.
- In rural Sub-Saharan Africa millions of people share their domestic water sources with animals or rely on unprotected wells that are breeding grounds for pathogens.
- At any one time, close to half of all people in developing countries are suffering from health problems caused by poor water and sanitation. Together, unclean water and poor sanitation is the world's second biggest killer of children. It has been calculated that 443 million school days are lost each year to water-related illness.

The poor people experience the biggest brunt from water contamination and scarcity, (Beeson 2008). According to the World Health Organization there are about 1.1 billion people in developing nations still lacking safe drinking water and more than 2.4 billion people lacking access to improved sanitation (Sultana and Loftus 2012). As such, water-borne illnesses is the leading cause of infant mortality in developing nations; 2.5 million people die each year from a lack of clean drinking water and adequate sanitation devices and services—that is an average of about 6,800 people per day or five people per minute, (Sultana and Loftus, 2012). Almost 100 percent of North Americans have access to abundant clean drinking water in the home, in comparison to only 69 percent of Mexicans having such access; water rights are something many in the developed world may take for granted, as they are not yet necessarily being fully impacted, (Staddon, Appleby and Grant 2012).

Right to water and Women

Gender is defined and refers to the differences in socially constructed roles and opportunities associated with being a man or a woman. It is the interactions and social relations between men and women; and it also determines expectations, permitted behavior and how both men and women are individually valued in a determined environment. Gender Approach allows for a theoretical and methodological analysis of gender relations to occur, thus enabling deeper understanding of gender dynamics in specific contexts, such as water scarcity and lack of access to water, which consequently helps build opportunity to promote equity (Aguilar 2009).

Women and men differ in the ways they manage environmental resources as well as they are also differentially affected by the degradation of natural resources, such as deforestation, water scarcity, water-related risks and so on. Because of their socially-constructed roles, women generally experience larger negative impacts from water-related risks than men due to their relative lack of resources, and reduced role in decision-making and capacity to take advantage of social, political and economic opportunities (Momsen 2004). It has long been recognised that women and girls, in both rural and urban areas, bear an inordinate responsibility for the collection of water for domestic purposes. The average distance that women in Africa and Asia walk to collect water is 6 kilometres. (Gideon et.al 2004) This inhibits women and girls' involvement in other activities such as education, income generation, cultural and political involvement, rest and recreation (Khosla et.al, 2003). Sanitation and hygiene tend to be women's responsibility, and women and girls also walk for hours to fetch drinking water. This not only takes time away from other tasks (such as education), but also exposes them to possible violence and health hazards (IFAD, 2007). Poor sanitation services at schools, for instance, may restrict young girls attending class whilst menstruating. About one in ten school-age African girls does not attend school during menstruation, or drops out at puberty because of the lack of clean and private sanitation facilities.(https://www.sswm.info). Gender equality is thus intrinsically linked to finding lasting solutions to poverty and injustice, considering it is estimated that women make up 70 per cent of the global poor. (AWRF Working Paper-4)

A gender analysis helps identify ways in which the health impacts of water resources affect women and men, girls and boys differently. For example, eye infections are particularly common in water scarce areas, where inability to maintain good hygiene is an important factor in blindness and trachoma in children. Blindness also affects the children's main carers who come into close contact with the infec-tions, and this is thought to be why blindness disproportionately affects women worldwide (Khosla and Pearl, 2003). Malaria, a water-related disease that causes widespread morbidity and mortality in Africa, dis-proportionately affects women during pregnancy. Pregnant women with malaria are more likely to develop anaemia, which leads to higher risk of maternal death. Infants born to mothers with malaria are likely to have low birth weight and thus be vulnerable to other infections and diseases. Girls and women head-load water, this can have very negative health effects on them. The energy consumption involved in water collection can have negative impacts on people with poor nutritional intake (Edwina Sandys, 2005).

Women are also often concerned with child safety in toilets. Cultural perceptions of decency related to sanitation facilities may also be gender specific. For example, in some cultures women would be reluctant to use toilets when the design allows their feet to be seen under a door or where they can openly be seen entering the toilet. It may also be considered inappropriate for a woman to share a toilet with her father-in-law. Such insensitive design may discourage women from toilet use. All too often, school-girls have been allocated the task of cleaning the toilets, a job that not only reproduced inequitable divisions of labour, but sometimes has rendered them more vulnerable to rape and sexual assault. Examples are reported of girls not using school toilets that they perceive as dirty and dangerous. (Edwina Sandys, 2005). A survey of 5 000 schools in Senegal showed that over half had no water supply and almost half had no sanitation facilities. Of those schools with sanitation, only half had separate facilities for boys and girls. The result was that girls chose not to utilise these facilities, either because they did not want to risk being seen to use the toilet, or because they were warned that these facilities were not private or clean enough. Girls also avoided drinking water at school to avoid urination, thereby becoming dehydrated and unable to concentrate (www.wateraid.org)

Already in 1992, the central role of women in water management was recognized in the Dublin Principles (adopted at the International Conference on Water and the Environment, Dublin). Since then, policymakers have made attempts to incorporate gender issues in water development projects.

But gender differentiation in irrigation management exists in many countries where women play a significant (or increasingly dominant) role in irrigated agriculture but are not well represented in management structures (e.g. water user associations) or in technical training (GWA 2003; Zwarteveen 1994). In contrast to the domestic sphere, in rural areas men tend to be seen as having primary responsibility for agricultural-water use and are often over-represented in formal resource agencies and irrigation management bodies (AWRF Working Paper). This is despite women playing significant roles in agriculture, as labourers and also in regards to household gardens and livestock. The under-representation of women in formal water resources management has direct gender impacts, as planning for water resources developments tends to prioritise activities where men are seen to have a dominant role. Water supply for rice production, for instance, may be prioritised over other productive uses such as household gardens and livestock, which women may have greater responsibility for. This may result in women having to rely on manual transportation of water for gardens, orchards and livestock, thus increasing their burden of responsibility (AWRF Working Paper).

Access to water and access to land, control of resources, and social networks are directly proportional. Such access is often more favourable for men than women. Women's limited access to water is also often coupled with their limited access to land; the two are often linked (IFAD 2001). Male biases in labour market regulation, in property rights and inheritance laws continue to restrict and shape the activities of women (GWA, 2003). Women are not only excluded in water resource management at the community level, but their participation in public spaces within the village is also very limited. However, despite the role that women play in reducing food insecurity through their knowledge of crop production, local biodiversity, soils and local water resources, they are often excluded from decision-making processes in new agricultural water management approaches and other projects and initiatives on natural resource allocation (IFAD, 2007). This means that women have no choice in the kind or location of services they receive. Women, who are already burdened with numerous duties attached to their multiple roles as workers, mothers, wives, daughters, housewives, carers etc., may see opportunities for them to participate in committees and decision making forums as yet another burden imposed on their busy lives. Therefore, participation cannot be seen in isolation from these wider processes, and the creation of opportunities for women's participation needs to also offer some relief for women from their heavy workload. This can be done through practical measures such as care in selection of the time meetings are held, the provision of crèches at committee meetings, and payment of sitting fees.

The influence of neoliberalism and the search for finance for water resource developments (especially in developing countries) has seen an increase in private sector involvement in water resources management as well as the increased application of market mechanisms for water allocation. A consequence of privatisation has been the increased attention on equity issues in water matters. Private property regimes tend to perpetuate and can even intensify gender inequalities. Women are often marginalized in monetary economy, and thus suffer when a price is put on water. Willingness-to-pay is not the same as the ability-to-pay; such assessments do not take into account the choices that poor women must make. Domestic or "reproductive" uses of water do not generate income directly, so benefits are not captured in traditional economic indicators (Liu, Julian). Women have been the most adversely affected by these increases [in water prices]. There are several reasons that account for this. First and foremost is the question of gender inequity and the asymmetrical power relations that deprive women of resources while assigning them the most menial, difficult and unrewarding jobs and roles. In most cases power at the household level is concentrated in the hands of men. Men care little about water bills and how and where the water is obtained (Amenga-Etego, Rudolf).

In an almost orchestrated format, the World Bank aligned with the United Nations (through the Dublin Principles), and the Kyoto Declaration in 2003, to push forward the consensus that the private sector was best placed to run the water systems in the global South; and corporations were recognized to operate in developing poor nations because they were best suited to aid these nations in providing fair access. On the other side, the global North remains safe and comfortable in all aspects. Governments in poor developing nations took in these recommendations and adopted them as part of their country's development programs, (Barlow 2007). What would occur next was not entirely what these institutions and water companies expected; they had severely neglected poor communities and the impact of privatization on poor women; water had now become an economic commodity which only those who could afford it would be able to purchase it. This would create massive controversy among these nations. Most significantly these protests are carried out by women in these countries. This is simply because of the overburden on the shoulders of women due to privatisation of natural resources, especially water. While women play a critical role in the water sector, they are rarely integrated into actual practice or policy. Some women tried to form local associations that work with their own locality. They have mobilized neighborhoods, municipalities and other partners to build water tanks, and have generated funds locally to pay for them (Case of Water Privatisation in Kenya). In Philippines' National Rural Women's Congress, attended by 280 participants from rural women's organizations, called for increased access to water services as a human right. The Rural Women's Congress also advocated the active participation of women in water supply development projects.

Water struggles

That Latin America is famous for its natural water repositories and it should have one of the highest per capita allocations of water in the world. But due to inequalities, polluted water and water privatization, it hasn't have enough water. Naturally the situation awakens protests from the local communities. Mexico and Bolivia have been particularly involved in massive movements to eradicate privatization to claim water rights as both human rights and as a source of livelihood (Paola, 2012). Poor women and in this case, poor urban women became by default the protagonists due to the direct impact they experience during inadequate water services; this is because, "...women's needs are inadequately represented or addressed by formal political institutions such as political parties...[consequently] protest has become the public voice of poor urban women," (Bennett 2000).

One of the largest and most well-known anti-privatization events in Latin America is the 'water war' of Cochabamba of 2000. During the protests in April 2000, women from the irrigation organizations defended their right to water, the right of the community to use water, their recognition as those responsible for acquiring the resource, the unity of their organizations and their acceptance as leaders. They also raised gender inequality issues in water management and demanded for greater participation, recognition, and decision-making power. Their reflections about the practices of exclusion and the mechanisms that make women invisible have given these members of irrigation organizations a double challenge: maintaining their already achieved social victories and broadening their participation and rights as women. Many times, women were at the head of the street actions in order to appeal to the police as women and mothers: "By chance were you not born of a woman? Didn't you grow in water? Don't you guys drink water? Do you not care? What you are doing?" (Beltrán - ý2004).

In India, Plachimada a tribal hamlet in Perumatty panchayat in Palakkad district of Kerala was in news for its struggle for water. This area of Palakkad has been facing severe water stress for quite some time. Just about six months after the Coca-Cola factory in Plachimada was set up in early 2000, villagers and farmers living nearby the bottling unit started noticing changes in both the quantity and quality of the well water. The water turned brackish and milky white and no longer fit for drinking, cooking and bathing (Nair,2015). The struggle against the Plachimada plant of Coca-Cola was launched on 22 April 2002, with a symbolic blockade and picketing by mainly the adivasis, particularly by women and children of the Malasar communities classified by the government as primitive tribes. Women in a small Indian hamlet in Kerala were able to force the Coca-Cola plant to shut down. "When you drink Coke, you drink the blood of people," said Mylamma, the woman who started the movement against Coca-Cola in Plachimada (Vandana Shiva, 2006). Later several others joined the protest. Majority of them were rural women. The court supported the women's demands and issued an order on 16th December 2003, ordering Coca-Cola to stop pirating ground water in Plachimada. The 12-year-old case finally reached closure after much wrangling, when Coca-Cola relinquished its license, stating in the SC that it did not intend to resume production from Plachimada. (The Hindu, 2017)

Privatisation of water that is fundamental to the existence of life on earth would lead to rise in what many scholars call as hydrological poverty or water poverty. Further it is reasonable to ask if the victims of water poverty really deserve to suffer. Commodification of water resource cannot be justified at any point in time. Due to the fundamental nature of water as the sustainer of both human life and the health of ecosystems, civil society groups have argued that its management should be kept in the public domain, so that governments can ensure universal access. The privatisation of water rights occurs when water entitlements are separated from land, have an economic value placed on them and are traded in a water market. In situations of water scarcity, the introduction of such changes assumes water will flow to more profitable uses. The concern is that water could 'flow uphill to money', as water rights are separated from their social and ecological context, and subject to market signals.

In 1992 at the Dublin Conference on Water and the Environment, four principles were adopted, in which one focused its attention on women and their role in the provision, management and safe guarding of water. This principle recognizes an important reality, which is that women are and have been central to water management. However, integrating a gendered perspective to water management—although crucial for sustainable development—has not been successfully implemented. The Dublin Conference declared water should be recognized as an economic good instead of a common good. Interestingly, in July 2010 the United Nations General Assembly adopted the human right to water; however, how it has been implemented, negotiated and experienced has remained a challenge, given water's new economic value.

The fact is that close to half of all people in developing countries suffer from health problems caused by poor water and sanitation. One of the main reasons for child mortality in the world is unclean water and poor sanitation. Women manage water resources not only for productive uses, but also for domestic purposes. Sanitation and hygiene for good health are their responsibility, and they often play an active role in the construction and preventive maintenance and repair of sanitation facilities. Women and girls also walk for hours to fetch drinking water. On the one hand, this fosters social and group cohesion and provides women with an opportunity to communicate with other women and people outside their homes. On the other hand, it exposes them to threats of violence and to health hazards. It also takes time away that might be used for more productive activities. Because of the socially-constructed roles and domestic responsibilities women generally experience larger negative impacts from water-related risks than men due to their relative lack of resources, and reduced role in decision-making and capacity to take advantage of social, political and economic opportunities. The recognition of water as a human right and public good is considered crucial to addressing the severe inequalities of access to water, as it impels governments under international law to meet their responsibility to respect, fulfill and protect people's right to water and improve the provision of water for essential needs.

It is widely recognized that water underpins economic development and social wellbeing. Water is essential for food and energy production, and serves as a necessary and often irreplaceable input in a wide variety of human actions. Conflicts over water are bound to increase if the precious good is not allowed to be shared equitably among communities and populations. It is therefore essential to evolve a notion of water democracy among the stakeholders.

Reference

Aguilar Lorena (2009) **Training Manual on Gender and Climate Change**, Union for Conservation of Nature (IUCN) and the United Nations Development Program (UNDP)

Amenga-Etego, Rudolf, Water Privatization in Ghana: Women's Rights Under Siege, Integrated Social and Development Centre, ACCRA-Ghana accessed from http://www.isodec.org.gh on 18/09/17.

Bakker Karen (2012) Commons Versus Commodities, Debating The Human Right to Water In The Right to Water: Politics, Governance and Social Struggles, ed. Farhana Sultana, and Alex Loftus, New York, Earthscan.

Bakker, Karen J. (2010) Privatizing Water: Governance Failure and the World's Urban Water Crisis, Ithaca, Cornell University Press.

Barlow Maude. (2007) Blue Covenant the Global Water Crisis and the Coming Battle for the Right to Water. New York: New Press.

Barlow, M. and T. Clarke (2003), Blue Gold: The Fight to Stop the Corporate Theft of the World's Water, New Delhi, LeftWord.

Beeson, Bart (2008), New Wave of Water Movement in Latin America, North American Congress on Latin America. Accessed from https://nacla.org on 27/09/17.

Beltrán Elizabeth Peredo (2004), Water, Privatization and Conflict: Women from the Cochabamba Valley accessed from http://www.boell.de on 10/10/17

Bennett Vivienne. (2000) Women and Urban Protest in Monterrey, Mexico, In Women and Water Management: The Latin American Experience, ed. Cecilia Tortajada, Oxford, Oxford University Press.

Equity Implications of Market and Property Rights Mechanisms: gender, Poverty and Indigenous Dimensions, AWRF Working Paper accessed from http://sydney.edu.au on 8/10/17

Gender and Water accessed from http:// www.ianas.org on 15.10/17

Gideon Burrows, Jules Acton and Tamsin Maunder (2004) Water and Sanitation: The education drain – A Water Aid Report, accessed from http://www.wateraid.org on 10/12/2016.

Goldman, M. (2007) How 'Water for all!' policy became hegemonic: The power of the World Bank and its transnational policy networks, Geoforum accessed from http://www.academia.edu on 03/10/17.

Grusky, S. (2002), Profit Stream: The World Bank and Greedy Global Water Companies, A Special Report by Public Citizen's Water for All Programme, U.S.A.

Gutierrez, E., Calaguas, B., Green, J. and Roaf, V. (2003) New Rules, New Roles: Does PSP Benefit the Poor?, Synthesis Report, London, WaterAid and Tearfund.

GWA (Gender and Water Alliance), accessed from http:/www .genderandwateralliance.org on 25/09/17.

Harris, L. (2009). Gender and Emergent Water Governance: Comparative Overview of Neoliberalized Natures and Gender Dimensions of Privatization, Devolution, and Marketization, Gender, Place and Culture Vol. 16, No. 4, August 2009, accessed from http://www.academia.edu on 03/10/17

Human Rights Council (2007) 'Report of the United Nations High Commissioner for Human Rights' on the *Scope and Content of the Relevant Human Rights Obligations Related to Equitable Access to Safe Drinking Water and Sanitation under International Human Rights Instruments,* Sixth Session', UN.

IFAD (2001) Rural Poverty Report 2001: The Challenge of Ending Rural Poverty, UK, Oxford University Press.

International Fund for Agricultural Development IFAD. (2007), Gender and Water: Securing water for improved rural livelihoods: The multiple-uses system approach,. Rome: IFAD,

Khosla, Prabha and Rebecca Pearl. (2003) Untapped Connections: Gender, Water and Poverty: Key Issues, Government Commitments and Actions for Sustainable Development, New York: WEDO.

Kothari, S. and I. Ahmad (2003) Nature as Value: Ecological Politics in India, In S. Kothari, I. Ahmad and H. Reifeld (eds.) The Value of Nature: Ecological Politics in India. U.P, India, Rainbow Publishers

Liu Julian, Human Rights and Gender Inequity in Water Resource Management, Centre for Economic & Social Rights. http://www.cesr.org on 18/09/17.

Meiyoshi Acabal Masgon, Robert Gensch, Water, Sanitation and Gender accessed from https://www.sswm.info on 25/01/17.

Momsen, Janet Henshall, (2004), Gender and Development, London, Routledge.

Nair Muraleedharan, UPDATED: JULY 15, 2017 16:49 IST

Ng, Cecilia (2000) Globalisation and Women, paper presented at Christian Conference of Asia, Kuala Lumpur, October 2000

Panda Smita Mishra, Privatisation of Water: Towards an Understanding of Gender Dimensions accessed from http://cutm.ac.in on 03/10/17.

Paola J. Canales, B.A. (2012) Women and Water: Gender, Privatization, And Water Rights in Latin America, Unpublished Thesis, Georgetown University Washington, D.C., accessed from https://repository.library.georgetown.edu on 15/10/17.

Peterson L.E. (2009) Human Rights and Bilateral Investment Treaties: Mapping the Role of Human Rights Law within Investor State Arbitration, Montreal, Canada: Rights and Democracy

Petrella, R. (2001) The Water Manifesto: Arguments for a World Water Contract, London, Zed Books.

Sandys Edwina (2005), Women and Water - the United Nations, United Nations Division for the Advancement of Women Department of Economic and Social Affairs accessed from http://www.un.org on 2/10/17

Shiva Vandana (2002) Water Wars: Privatization, Pollution and Profit, Cambridge, South End Press

Shiva Vandana (2006), Resisting Water Privatisation, Building Water Democracy, A paper on the World Water Forum in Mexico City accessed from http://www.globalternative.org on 16/10/17.

Staddon, Chad, Thomas Appleby, and Evadne Grant (2012) A Right to Water? Geographico-legal Perspectives, In The Right to Water: Politics, Governance and Social Struggles, ed. Farhana Sultana, and Alex Loftus, New York, Earthscan.

Sultana, Farhana, and Alex Loftus, eds. (2012), **The Right to Water: Politics, Governance and Social Struggles,** New York, Earthscan.

UNDP (2006), **Human Development Report 2006. Beyond Scarcity: Power, Poverty And The Global Water Crisis,** UNDP.

United Nations (2002), *Substantive Issues Arising in the Implementation of the International Covenant on Economic, Social and Cultural Rights: General Com*ment No. 15 (2002): The Right to Water (Arts. 11 and 12 of the International Covenant on Economic, Social and Cultural Rights), 29th Sess., U.N.

United Nations (2013), We Can End Poverty; Millennium Development Goals and beyond 2015 accessed from http://www.un.org on 27/09/17.

United Nations Development Programme (UNDP, 2006), Human Development Report 2006- Beyond Scarcity: Power, poverty and the global water crisis accessed from http://hdr.undp.org on 23/09/17.

United Nations Educational, Scientific and Cultural Organization (UNESCO, 2009), UNESCO Etxea - UNESCO Centre Basque Country Outcome of the International Experts' Meeting on the Right to Water. Paris, 7 and 8 July 2009 accessed from www.http://unesdoc.unesco.org on 23/09/17.

United Nations Human Settlements Programme (UN-HABITAT), Centre on Housing rights and Evictions (COHRE), American Association for the Advancement of Science (AAAS), Swiss Agency for Development and Cooperation (SDC), Manual on the Right to Water and Sanitation. 2007 accessed from http://www.unhabitat.org on 23/09/17.

Water Wars: Plachimada vs Coca-Cola, The Hindu, July 15, 2017

Whose Water? A Study of the Struggle for Water at Plachimada, Kerala accessed from http://www.inflibnet.ac.in on 16/10/17.

Women in Development Europe (WIDE) (2004) Water is a Common Good, Belgium, Network Women in Development Europe.

World Health Organization (WHO, 2003), Office of the High Commissioner for Human Rights (OHCHR), Centre on Housing Rights and Evictions (COHRE), Water Aid, Centre on Economic, Social and Cultural Rights, The Right to Water. 2003, accessed from .http://www2.ohchr.org on 23/09/17.

World Health Organization (WHO, 2010), The Right to Water, Fact Sheet No. 35 accessed from http://www.ohchr.org on 23/09/17.

Zwarteveen, M (1994) Gender Issues, Water Issues: A Gender Perspective to Irrigation Management, Working Paper, Colombo, IWMI.

9

Human Security Concerns and Gender Reflections on Climate Change

—*Anjali Devi. M*

Climate change poses a serious threat to the very survival of mankind and environment in the contemporary times. The adverse effects of it have asymmetrical impact on developed and developing countries as well as on men and women. As compared to developed countries, insufficient financial infrastructure coupled with poor adaptation and mitigation facilities makes the developing states more vulnerable to the vagaries of nature. Similarly women are more affected due to changing climatic patterns. They become vulnerable in two ways: they are susceptible as women and they are vulnerable for being part of a community. While drought makes them to walk miles and miles to fetch water, flood makes them stranded due to patriarchal and gender restrictions. This article tries to contextualise how the alterations in the climate and environment further intensified the susceptibility of women.

Key words: women, climate change, vulnerability, developing countries, GSDRR

"Women are more likely to die in natural disasters"

(The Sydney Morning Herald 2015)

Background

The growing instances of environmental degradation and subsequent natural calamities forced the international community to revisit the utilitarian notion of using environment. Millions of people lost their life and livelihood and majority of them displaced as environmental refugees which became a major question before the states. This crucial political situation made them to initiate thorough discussions on sustainable ways of utilising environment. The deliberations over these years also brought out the increasing plight of women and the marginalised sections of society during the changing climatic conditions. Climate change and its impacts on society and environment became serious concerns even after and found its place in the United Nations Conference on Human Environment held at Stockholm (1972). The Stockholm Conference called for an international cooperation to resolve the present environmental crisis and also chalked out various measures to contain it. The declaration says "Man has the fundamental right to freedom, equality and adequate conditions of life, in an environment of a quality that permits a life of dignity and well-being".

Concerns about climate change and its aftermath was reinstated in the United Nations Conference on Environment and Development, widely known as Earth Summit in 1992 and resulted in the creation of an Inter-governmental Panel on Climate Change. This was followed by international Conferences on Population and Development (1994), World Conference on Women (1995), Hyogo Conference (2005) etc. One could witness a radical shift in the security studies from military to non-military threats. The need to address and contain non-military threats has become very conspicuous because of its trans-national nature. Among the non-military threats climate change induced natural disasters are more alarming since the economic costs and human casualties inflicted by these threats are irreparable in nature.

The Inter-governmental Panel for Climate Change (IPCC) has defined climate change as "any change in climate over time, whether due to natural variability or as a result of human activity" (IPCC 2007). Scientific evidences around the world shows anthropogenic activities including greenhouse gas emissions (GHG) are mainly responsible for the changing climatic conditions. The IPCC in its fifth assessment report (AR5) states that annual temperature across the globe has shot up to almost a degree in the last century; sea level has risen in many parts of the World while the snow and ice cover has also deteriorated alarmingly. The report also observed that number of warmer days in a year increased and at the same time the cold days and nights shows a decreasing tendency. It further maintains that atmospheric concentrations of greenhouse gases have risen since 1750 due to anthropogenic activities (IPCC 2014). Unpredictable flood, drought, sea water intrusion, avalanches, Glacial Lake Outburst Flood (GLOF) etc apparent are examples of changing climatic patterns. Variations in temperature and unpredictable downpour affect the food production of majority countries results in the food insecurity. Retreating of glaciers and drying up of rivers further aggravates the problem. The epidemics spreading after each natural disaster causes heath insecurity of people. Climate change particularly rapid-onset of events, may result in death, injury or damage to health through an increase in infectious diseases, physical and mental stress and the loss of bio-diversity. In several regions it has reached to the extent of affecting the economic growth of the country and stands as a major hurdle in attaining the Millennium Development Goals (MDGs) particularly eradication of poverty and hunger and ensuring environmental sustainability (UN 2015).

The global effects of climate change will negatively impact communities and groups at multiple levels, threatening the security, economic and human rights conditions of the people around the world. Women are disproportionately burdened and affected by these processes due to multiple factors, but at the same time they also have the capacity to lead adaptation and create more resilient communities. Women are deprived of political and economic power and they have limited access to financial and material resources particularly during conflict-affected, post-conflict or less economically developed settings; which can further exacerbate their vulnerability towards climate change.

The Convention on the Elimination of All Forms of Discrimination against Women (CEDAW), 1979 provides a framework for linking climate change with the protection of women from harms emanated from environmental degradation. The Beijing Platform for Action, 1995 made detailed discussions on climate change and emphasised the role of women's decision making in protecting the environment. The sustainable development goals (SDGs) officially known as Transforming our World: the 2030 Agenda for Sustainable Development has mentioned gender equality and climate action as their main agenda. The United Nations Security Council Resolution (1325) adopted in 2000 was yet another document reinforces climate change and women empowerment from a security standpoint. The International Bar Association in a report stated the relationship between international law and climate change: "Gender equity is also an essential element of climate change justice....As climate change accelerates migration and displacement, women in particular are subject to abuse and deprivation"

The German Advisory Council on Global Change in its report (2007) identifies four key variables that are likely to cause violent conflict, political upheaval and humanitarian crises in the future: food insecurity, natural disasters, water scarcity and migration due to environmental degradation.

Middle East, North Africa, Central Asia, the Pacific Rim and the Mediterranean along with certain countries like Bangladesh are the most vulnerable countries towards climate change. Coincidentally these are the regions having gender gaps in different social development indicators including health, education, political participation and economic participation.

Although climate change is a borderless phenomenon and it affects people across the globe, one cannot deny the fact that women are the worst sufferers of climate change, especially those in the Global South. An average 43% of the global agricultural workforce is women and women farmers produce 90 per cent of African continent's food supply. Failure to address women's concerns while formulating climate change policy will have serious repercussions in the global food security. Emmeline Skinner notes that since women and girls are predominantly in charge of unpaid household chores in less economically developed countries, especially in rural areas "their lives are directly affected by the changing climatic conditions". Their domestic duties require more time due to climate change induced water shortages, deforestation which severely curtailed their mobility and heightened their hardships. Recent researches from different parts of the world clearly reveal that the scarcity of natural resources due to environmental degradation affects the schooling and working conditions of women.

Impact of climate change on women

It is beyond any doubt that climate change and consequent natural disasters have disproportionate effect on the women and children in society. Women and children are fourteen times more likely to die in the natural disasters than men. The drought of 1999 and 2000 in Balochistan displaced thousands of people. Among them women and children were the worst sufferers (Hanif 2012). Many factors including social, economic, gender and economic constraints are responsible for the vulnerability of women to climate change. On this backdrop the article is trying to identify hurdles faced by women to combat climate change and reasons for high death rate of women in natural disasters.

One of the major impacts of climate change on women is that it increases their workload. Lack of fresh water and search for firewood has affected women and girls alike as they have to travel long distance to fetch water and cooking fuel. The reports from Ethiopia, one of the least developed countries of the World states that time to fetch water has increased by at least four hours per day. Walking long distance deteriorates health conditions of women in general and hampers the success rate of school going girls in particular resulting in their drop out. When there is shortage of food during flood and drought, women feeds the men in the home first and they eat the left outs. This affects the nutritional level of women making them more vulnerable to climate change. These facts reveal that majority of men willingly or unwillingly harm the women and reduce their welfare (Swarup 2011).

After each natural catastrophe, the death toll of women is high compared to men. When cyclone Sidr hit Bangladesh in 1991, it took a death toll of 138,000 (Bern 1993). Among them the mortality rate of women over the age of forty was thirty one per cent. In the Asian tsunami of 2004, more than seventy per cent of dead were women. Hurricane Katrina that struck United States of America in 2005 predominantly affected the African-American women who are the marginalised sections of the then society. These case studies reiterate that despite of being a developed or developing country the poor and marginalised sections of the society are the major victims of natural disasters. Recent researches conducted by the London School of Economics (LSE) by taking a sample of 141 countries from 1981-2002 finds that natural disasters kill more women than men or kill women at earlier stage than men. Different factors including biological and physiological differences, social norms and role behaviour and discrimination in access to resources and breakdown of social order are responsible for this. (Neumayer and Plumper 2007)

One of the important concerns due to rising sea level is the increased salinity. Women have to face adverse effect of this especially in area where they are cultivators. The government of Bangladesh and Caritas Development Institute reported a range of health problems among coastal populations especially women due to increased salinity through drinking, cooking and bathing leading to hypertension and miscarriage among women, skin diseases including cancer, acute pulmonary disorders and diarrhoeal diseases (Vinies 2011). In the African country of Senegal, various NGOs and organisations joined hands to construct a 3,300 meter anti-salt dyke to repossess lands affected by saline water intrusion. This activity of NGOs leads to revitalization of rice growing activities. This has also regenerated natural vegetation and promoted biodiversity recovery (Alam 2015).

Flood is a crucial natural disaster that makes the otherwise peaceful atmosphere upside down. Women and girls are the principal victims of this. The case of Pakistan during the super floods of 2010 is as an example of this. The studies make visible that women who were pregnant who were caught in the floods were died or became disabled due to pregnancy related complications. Several cases of female adolescent marriage have been reported during this period. Fears of sexual assault, sexual harassment, rape etc. have forced many of the girls for early marriages. 172 cases of rape have been reported in the province of Sindh alone during 2008-2011(Bukahri and Rizvi 2015). One of the studies relates floods and women in Bangladesh, found cultural values as a main hindrance for them to reach relief camps. Unequal food distribution, lack of relief operations, obedience to male members, self-sacrifices etc. make rural Bangladeshi women more vulnerable to flood and other natural calamities (Haqque 1996)

On the other hand forests constitute an important source for food, firewood, timber, material for crafts, animal fodder and medicinal herbs etc for a large section of society principally women. Minor forest products are collected normally by women. As climate change occurs, men moves to distant urban areas in search of livelihood. Consequently women have to make extra effort to secure resources and feed their families. In most of the cases women serve as the manager of household resources and their burdens are likely to become significantly heavier as they must find new sources of food and resources to support their families, travelling farther and spending more time addressing the resources scarcity. Protection of land and afforestation has the capacity to help community and women in their mitigating efforts.

Ocean acidification is the change in the chemistry of ocean due to emission of carbon dioxide. Ocean acidification leads to coral bleaching- a condition that occurs when warm waters cause coral polyps to expel the symbiotic algae that give them colour. Ocean acidification affects the fisheries as well. When the production of fish diminishes, the availability of fish and sea food also diminishes. Even though the relation between ocean acidification and women are understudied, fish as a resource will dwindle and livelihoods will be threatened.

The Water Project 2015 is a report of how the scarcity of water affects society in general and women in particular. It says that approximately one billion people are affected by water scarcity. Scarcity of water can be defined as the lack of access to clean and healthy drinking water. Developing and underdeveloped countries are the worst affected by water scarcity. Among them women is more vulnerable due to water scarcity. Many reasons contribute to this like they need to travel miles and miles to fetch water. Variations in temperature pattern, rainfall, solar radiation and wind increases the desertification of land. Water scarcity affects the agricultural patterns and it affects the food production adversely. The impact of desertification and drought can include the loss of livelihoods and displacement of population from one degraded ecosystem zone to another.

Women who belong to a major agricultural force are affected drastically due to desertification and water scarcity. Water scarcity compels men to migrate in search of green pastures. Subsequently, women take the responsibility of household but with less decision making powers, community services, education and financial resources. In addition to this, there will be laws that prevent them from being able to acquire, own and retain land or other assets. These circumstances compel women to increase petty trade and prostitution which also increase the risk of HIV/AIDS. The National Human Rights Commission of Nepal is of the opinion that human trafficking especially of women and children have increased by 15 per cent after the Nepal earthquake of 2015. The statistics shows that in three months after the earthquake, 331 persons of less than 18 years of age and 394 persons of over 18 years were intercepted (Khan 2016).

Lack of access to potable water affects women adversely than men. In communities where irrigation is a distant dream and clean water is a precious commodity, women and girls bear the primary burden of finding the drinking water. A report by the World Health Organisation reiterates that globally, women and children collectively spend 200 million hours per day collecting water for their families and communities resulting in lost productive potential. This time could have spent for attending schools/ colleges or income generating jobs (UNICEF 2016). Travelling long distance in search of water and sanitation increases the risk of sexual violence. This is particularly true for the countries which lie in the conflicts zone. Eliasson discusses a case of a girl in North East Uganda. She is frequently threatened by men and boys with extreme form of sexual violence and even death on her way to collect water in the early morning. The girl also narrated a case where her friend became pregnant after such an attack (Eliasson 2011). UKaid mentions that there is a link between access to water and sanitation facilities and increasing sexual violence against women (Lennon 2011).One of the report says that in conflict zones majority of the rapes occur while women goes out for collecting water, firewood etc. Women in Democratic Republic of Congo reported that they are often attacked by armed assailants and often wearing military uniforms (Makisaka 2011). Access to clean drinking water reduces the incidence of rape and abduction and it also helps to fulfil the productive potential of women like realizing education attainment and economic empowerment. Health and sanitation is the other major factor that is at risk due to water scarcity. Women and girls need to compromises hygiene especially the poor. Mostly women need water for the purpose uncommon to men, particularly during menstruation and pregnancy (United Nations 2006).

In most of the societies men are better equipped to combat the vulnerabilities of climate change than that of women. If women have not been taught swimming, there are more chances of her being washed away due to her fragile body compared to men. The risk increases in case of a pregnant woman as her mobility is restricted. Social infrastructure is the first 'causality' in a disaster stricken country. Inaccessibility to food, water, hygiene, health services etc. results in communicable diseases which make women and children more vulnerable. As mentioned elsewhere, when there is shortage of food and water, women feed men first. Bias in the social structure towards female children during natural calamities can be substantiated by a striking example. A Chinese peasant woman reveals that during the famine of 1960s families tried to pool their ratios and often the male members do not hesitate to say that let the female children die first. Furthermore, during the rescue operations there are chances of bias towards male and boys. An example of a father who was unable to hold his daughter and son together underlines the above statement. Since he could not hold both of the kids together, he left the girl reasoning that the boy has to take all the responsibilities of home and he has to do rituals of his parents after death (Bushra 2009). Incidences from different parts of the world make clear the strong bias towards men during the refugee operations and relief distribution. These instances reveals that rather than the biological and physiological differences it is the gender bias that makes women more susceptible to climate change induced natural disasters.

Social, religious and cultural norms also make women vulnerable to climate change. In most of the countries the role of women is constrained to that of a care taker of children and elders. In majority of the cases, stereotypical role of women refrain them from going to schools making them illiterate and compels them to work in informal sector. In addition to this, women have unequal access to resources and decision making process. In Pakistan, women being the main providers of food, face difficulty in accessing land and resources. Sixty seven per cent of the women are engaged in the agricultural activities while only one per cent of them own their land. Moreover, socio-cultural norms restrict women from stepping out of their home even if natural disasters struck (Neumayer and Plumper 2007). In the rural areas of Bangladesh women are forced to wear *sari* which restrict their movement during natural calamities like flood. In addition to this, without the permission of the male head of the family, a female member cannot move away from home (UNESCO 2008). Consequently, even if an earthquake or natural disaster strikes, women have to wait until the arrival of male head of the family, to move away from affected areas. Social restrictions prohibit women from learning swimming or climbing a tree which could have helped them during calamities. Vulnerability of women is aggravated by the early warning systems (EWS) which are oriented towards men (World Bank 2003). Because of the early warning, men could take precautions; on the contrary, women have to live in darkness. These incidents point out the need for gender sensitive disaster risk reduction and disaster management techniques.

Need for gender neutral disaster risk reduction and disaster management

Despite of the susceptibility of women towards climate change, disaster management and risk reduction remains gender biased and not received any attention from the part of policy makers. The bias towards men and boys are visible even in the relief operations. The Pan-American Health Organisation states "the majority of relief efforts are intended for the entire population of a disaster affected area; however, when they rely on existing structures of resource distribution that reflects the patriarchal structure of society. Women are marginalized in their access to relief resources" (Bushra 2009). Despite of this in the temporary refugee camps, chances of sexual harassment makes women are more insecure. Climate change induced migration also affects women. While men can search for green pastures, women are stuck to their land whether it is undergoing deforestation, deluged with floods or droughts (Dutta 2015). In totality women are the unseen victims of climate wars and resource scarcity.

The latest report by *India today* titled "The tremor of trafficking" highlights the shocking incidences of human trafficking in the earthquake affected Nepal. The United Nations Population Fund reports that there are two million women and girls especially vulnerable in Nepal and among them 1.4 million are living in the crowded camps. Among them, at least 28,000 who lost their family are at the high risk of exploitation. These women and girls are trafficked for slavery and prostitution. The report further states 'immediately after the earth quake, the numbers of Nepali girls in Lucknow brothels have increased' (Dutta 2015). The immediate need of women in makeshift camps was *sindoor* not blankets. Women believe that if they have *sindoor* in their foreheads they can escape from sexual harassment, says one of the humanitarian forces. The recurrence of drought and poverty forced many of the young women to take up prostitution as a source of livelihood. Women have different needs especially when they are pregnant and lactating. Relief measures from the part of the state as well the voluntary organisations also do not reflect their needs. Saris are provided without petticoats in some cases (Gokhale 2008).

Women faces psychological breakdown after natural disasters. Psychological response of women to natural disasters can be classified as initial response and long term reactions. Immediately after a natural disaster, women reach a state of shock since they have seen their husbands and kids being washed away or seeing them buried under rubbles. As a result of shock they may keep mum for long time and might stop taking food. This mental state of women results in sleeping disorder. Women become sceptical of the security of children, husband and themselves after calamities. These thoughts provoke anxiety which make day to day life ordeal. Women also find difficulty in getting legal help for compensation, providing food for their children and sending children to schools. These all adds to distress of women after each natural catastrophe (Augliar 2012). These all underlines the need to mainstream gender in disaster management and disaster risk reduction process of each region.

Women have distinguished ability to adapt to environmental degradation. As most affected due to climate change, they should be at the centre in framing solutions in adapting to climate change. Community based programmes with women at the core has been initiated in some areas of the world. Women in rural communities of Ganga river basin of Nepal, India and Bangladesh have started cultivating flood and drought resistant food crops. The active role of women in disaster risk reduction can be highlighted with the example of La Masica municipality, Honduras. Women have been taking proactive role under the programme "Garifuna Emergency Committee for Honduras" in response to disasters. Traditionally, responding to disasters is considered to be "male" dominant. When women were included as equal participants in disaster preparedness plans in this small town of La Masica, Honduras, no one has died even after the hurricane (Oxfam America 2009). The non-governmental organisation called 'Swayam Shiksha Prayog (learning from one's own and others experience)' based in Maharashtra has helped women in the resilience process after natural calamities. In 1993 Latur earthquake Swayam Shiksha Prayog trained women helped in repairing the damaged houses. The NGO has trained women to take their role as motivators, build technical capacity, demonstrate collective arrangements, provide feedback and monitor reconstruction. Gradually women have attained the capacity to initiate proactive role towards climate change induced natural disasters (Vasudha 2008). Despite of women being the most vulnerable section of population due to climate change, they are not proportionally represented in the climate change negotiations.

The gender composition of constitutional bodies established under convention and Kyoto Protocol in Conference of Parties 19 is as low as 13 per cent even though they constituted 33 per cent of the bureaux (UNFCCC 2013). There are examples were women are not even consulted in decision making process related to climate change. In the Kilombero district of Tanzania, a well built by a non-governmental organisation had dried up soon after its construction. When the volunteers of NGO talked to the community, they realised that it is the duty of women to dig the well and they know the places that better provide the water yields. Since this incident women have better involved in the decision making process of the community (Fisher 2006). The Potohar Organisation for Development Advocacy (PODA-Pakistan) is a non-governmental organisation working for women rights following natural disasters. At the international level also innovative measures has been taken place to increase women's voice in the decision making process. In 2009, Finland has provided five lakh Euros for the women of developing countries to participate in Conference of parties 2009 (Aira 2009). In the same year the Global Action on Gender Sensitive Disaster Risk Reduction that took place in Beijing has adopted a nine point strategy for mainstreaming gender concerns in the disaster reduction process (2009). These include:-

- Increase political commitment to gender analysis and gender mainstreaming through enhanced cooperation and collaboration.
- Develop and review national policies, relevant laws, strategies, plans, and budgets and take immediate action to mainstream gender into national development policies, planning and programmes.
- Foster the link[1]age between disaster risk reduction and climate change adaptation from a gender perspective through policy and administrative measures;
- Collect gender-specific data and statistics on impact of disasters, carry out gender-sensitive vulnerability, risk and capacity assessments and develop gender sensitive-indicators to monitor and measure progress;

- Increase awareness of the public and media on the gender-sensitive vulnerabilities and capacities in disasters and gender-specific needs and concerns in disaster risk reduction and management;
- Support research institutions to study the cost-benefit and efficiency of gender-sensitive policies and programmes in disaster risk reduction, climate change adaptation and poverty reduction;
- Secure the actual application of disaster risk assessments as part of development policy-making and programme formulation to prevent disasters from making the poor even poorer;
- Improve and mainstream a gender perspective and equal participation between men and women in the coordination of disaster preparedness, humanitarian response, and recovery through capacity building and training
- Build and enhance the capacities of professional organizations, communities and pertinent national and local institutions to enable gender mainstreaming into all development sectors.

In short, the United Nations and other institutions related to climate change should realise that women are not just victims of natural catastrophes; but have amazing potential for resilience capacity. They should initiate a global campaign with mainstreaming gender and they should also urge national governments to take decisions with women at the core. With high dependence on primary activities for their livelihood and their role play as care takers, women have conspicuous role to play in changing climatic conditions and natural catastrophes.

References

Alam, Mayesha et.al, 2015, "Women and climate change:Impacts and agency in human rights, security and development", Georgetown Institute of Peace and security.

Augliar, Lorena, 2012 "*Climate Change and disaster mitigation: gender makes difference*", International union for conservation of nature, Switzerland

Beijing Agenda for Global Action on Gender sensitive Disaster Reduction, Available at w ww.unisdr.org/files/8024_8961BeijingAgendafinal22Apr091.doc., Accessed on 2 August 2017

Bern *et.al.*(1993), *Risk factors for mortality in Bangladesh cyclone in 1991,* Bulletin of World Health Organisation,71(1):73-78.

Bukhari, Syed Iazaz Ahmad and Rizvi, Shahid Hassan, 2015, " Impact of Floods on Women: With Special Reference to Flooding: Experience of 2010 Flood in Pakistan", Geography and natural disasters

Climate Change 2007: Working Group 11: Impacts, Adaptation and Vulnerability. Available at http://www.ipcc.ch/publications_and_data/ar4/wg2/en/annexessglossary-a-d.html. Accessed on 13 October 2017

Climate Change and Millennium Development Goals 2015, Available at www.un-kampagne.de/.../final_MDG_Climate_Change_Brochure.pdf., Accessed on 1 August 2015

Karat, Climate change: women in the developing countries the hardest hit, 2011 Available at www.karat.org/wp-content/.../Brief-on-Gender-and-climate-change.pdf., Accessed on 6 August 2015

Datta Damayanti, 2015, "The tremor of trafficking", India Today, Available at http://indiatoday.intoday.in/story/the-tremor-of-trafficking/1/455225.html, Accessed on 4 August 2017

Eliasson, Jan, 2011, "Sexual Violence on the Way to Water", Available at http://www.huffingtonpost.com/jan-eliasson/sexual-violance-on-the-wa_b_832035.html, Accessed on 29 August 2017

Fisher, Julie, 2006, "For her it's a big issue: putting women at the centre of water supply, sanitation and hygiene. Evidence Report", Available at http://www.wsscc.org/sites/default/files/publications/wsscc_for_her_its_ the _ big_issue_evidence_report_2006_en.pdf., Accessed on 9 August 2016.

Gokhale, Vasudha, 2008, "Role of women in disaster management:an analytical study with reference to Indian society" Paper presented at the 14th world conference on earthquake engineering, Beijing, China.

Hanif, Shahina ed.(2012), Climate change and women: A *study of* selected sites in rural Pakistan-2011,Women's Resource Centre, Lahore.

IPCC 2014: Climate change 2014 synthesis report, IPCC, Geneva, Switzerland.

Kalela, Aira, 2009, "Women will make a difference", Available at http://issuu.com/nikk—nordic-gender-institute/docs/nikkmagasin_2-2009/17., Accessed on 9 August 2017.

Khaliq,Bushra, 2009, "Women's bodies in war,peace and climate change", available at http://www.isiswomen.org/phocadownload/print/isispub/wia/wia2009-2/2wia09_03talkpoints_bushra.pdf., Accessed on 21 May 2017

Khan, Hamza, 2016, "Nepal: 'Since earthquake, 15% spike in human trafficking', The New Indian Express

Khondker, Habibul Haque, 1996, "Women and floods in Pakistan", International Journal of mass emergencies and disasters, 14(3): 281-292

Neumayer,Eric and Plumper,Thomas (2007), The gendered nature of natural disasters: the impact of catastrophic events on the gender gap in the life expectancy ,1981-2002, *Annals of the Association of Geographers,* 97(3):551-566

Swarup, Anita et.al ,2011, *Weathering the storm: adolescent girls and climate change*, Plan, UK,London.

UNESCO report on "Gender and natural disasters", available at http://www.unesco.org/bpi/ppt/gender_2008_3forum_climate_sc_rouhban_en.ppt., Accessed on 15 July 2016

Vineis, Paola et.al, 2011 "Climate change impacts on water salinity and heath", Science Direct, 1(1): 5-10

World Bank, *Protecting new health facilities from natural disasters: guidelines for the promotion of disaster mitigation* 2003, Washington D.C.

10

Connecting the Disconnected': An Appraisal of New Social Media Interventions in Human Right Scenario

—Sabu Thomas

Introduction

The development of internet and allied technologies has made the world a connected world. The new digital technologies have reached every nook and corner of the globe and has extended to the length and breadth of social and political structures. The evolution of digital technologies has also altered the landscape of modern governance. The traditional patterns of governmental interactions, both in vertical and horizontal dimensions, were subjected to an unprecedented and unparalleled transformation. Government agencies and institutions were forced to adjust with the patterns of the newly evolved digital society. One of the major characteristics of the digital society is the extensive and deep rooted dependence on modern Information and Communication Technologies (ICTs)[1]. These technologies facilitate better communication with the governance systems and its stakeholders. This resulted in the development of a 'molecular democracy' (Anderson, 2010) which incidentaly changed the citizen- government relations. Molecular democracy assures more intimate and personal governance solutions that may extend even to the peripheries of society. The technologies also facilitated new venues of debate and platforms for interactions which accommodated most of the micro interests in the larger society (Coleman & Blumer, 2009).

In the course of time digital patterns of governance was well accepted by government entities all over the world[2]. They found it as a convenient and comfortable tool to deliver good governance and as a mechanism to assure legitimacy for the governing systems[3]. New patterns of governance provide for a Simple, Moral, Accountable, Responsive, and Transparent (SMART) service delivery system. Governmental procedures are straightened and simplified (Bingham, et.al., 2005, Dunleavy, et.al., 2005, Lane, 2009). The internet is also acting as an effective factor that drives global economy. Estimates put the Internet's contribution to global GDP at as much as $4.2 trillion in 2016[4]. The innovations of the technological revolution have ranged from three-dimensional technology to digital banking, from e-books to e-commerce, from the sharing economy to crowdworking. The economy was reconstructed in a peer to peer fashion with individualised and customised marketing and demand satisfaction.Traditional workplaces were redesigned to personal spaces that is flexible and more competetive and remunerative. Mobile phones and mobile Internet services offer many new opportunities for people —people that range from access to dynamic price information, productivity gains job creation in technology-based industries and labour-market services. The digital revolution raises the hope of addressing daunting challenges as ensuring food security, overcoming health concerns, combating climate change and meeting energy needs.

The new developments in ICTs also resulted in the development of new social media. The political spectrum also has undergone a vast change through the introduction of innovative technologies including social media. The political leaders and their constituency became more interactive and vibrant (Howard, et al. 2016). New forms of participation — particularly though social networks with global reach — are increasingly important in policymaking. They are based on fast and decentralized interactions (Jahan 2016). The new social media provided a large space for people to people and people to government communications. The monopoly of traditional media in the dissemination and distribution of public information was successfully broken. Government censoring and media restrictions were easily bypassed and the new news distribution pattern was also complimented with ever-growing number of audience which cut across borders and nationality. The arrival of electronic media for transmitting information altered the power equations in governance. The meaning of democracy is also being redefined. The many can now simultaneously 'speak' to the few in power, and derive the required response (Bedi et al. :2001). The internet revolution has made information much cheaper and accessible and this in turn had tremendous implications for the public sector and its organization. Another major implication of ICTs and new social media is its intervention in the protection of human rights. The new social media is currently an active agency for the promotion and protection of human rights all over the world. They open vibrant platforms for human right debates and movements. This may range from a revolution against oppressive regime to a local environment issue.

Global ICT Scenario

The creation of World Wide Web in 1990, by researchers at the European Laboratory for Particle Physics, Geneva, announced the beginning of a connected world. Within a short span of time these technologies gained unprecedented global acceptance. According to international Telecommunication Union (2016) seven billion people which come around 95% of the global population live in an area that is covered by a mobile-cellular network. Mobile-broadband networks reach 84% of the global population. Mobile penetration has reached saturation level in many countries and still grows 7.6% annually. This should also be read with accelerated shift to personalized digital technologies including mobile broadband connections and possession of smart phones.

Table 1: Global use of Internet (Area/Development wise distribution)

Sl. No.	*Area*	*Percentage*
1.	Europe	79.1
2.	The Americas	65.0
3.	CIS	66.6
4.	Arab States	41.6
5.	Asia& Pacific	41.9
6.	Africa	25.1
7.	World	47.1
8.	Developed World	81.0
9.	Developing World	41.0
10.	Least Developed World	15.2

(*Source:* Compiled from International Telecommunication Union ICT Facts and Figures 2016)

It was estimated that 47.1% of global population uses internet and related technologies. The usage in the developed world is 81% and it is 41% in developing areas. Only 15.2% of population in the least developed areas uses internet. In the internet usage statistics Europe occupies the top position with 79.1% of population using the technologies. Africa with 25.1%

population is the least winner. There is an evident gap in the usage of digital technologies across the globe and this creates a serious digital divide.

Mobile technology is becoming an affordable tool to fill in the digital gap between developed and developing countries, especially with the rapidly declining price of mobile products. Cost of digital tools and network connectivity is also rapidly decreasing while connectivity speed and technology advancements are witnessing phenomenal growth.

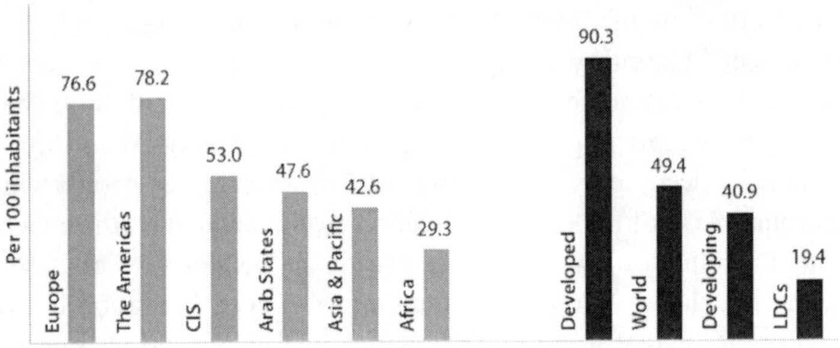

(*Source:* International Telecommunication Union ICT Facts and Figures 2016)

Figure Mobile Broad Band Subscriptions Area/Development wise figures (2016)

In developing countries, the number of mobile-broadband subscriptions continues to grow at double digit rates, reaching a penetration rate of close to 90.3%. The total number of mobile- broadband subscriptions is estimated to reach 3.6 billion by end 2016.The global average of mobile broad band subscription stands at 49.4% with developing countries holding 40.9% share and least developed countries having 19.4% share. The spread of mobile instruments and mobile technology bears a special significance in the debate on social media. The social media is personal and individual centric and as such they make use of portable communication tools. Most of the social media traffic emanates from personal devices.

The evolution of Social media

Social media is defined as "a group of Internet-based applications that build on the ideological and technological foundations of Web 2.0, and that allow the creation and exchange of User Generated Content[5]" (Joseph 2012). Social media is generally a bunch of innovative and interactive products. They include: collaborative projects, virtual worlds, blogs, content communities, and social networking. Collaborative projects mean people working together to create content. The best example is Wikipedia which is a collective attempt to store and disseminate information to global public at no cost. Blogs are personal websites. Individuals may interact with a blog by commenting on its content. Virtual worlds include virtual games or virtual social worlds such as Second Life. Content communities are sites where users can share content with other members of their online community. You tube is one example for content community. People also share information on social networking sites, of which Facebook and Twitter are the most popular.

In the earlier days of internet, social media innovations were limited by the nature of technologies and acceptance level. The Bulletin Board Systems of 70's can be considered as an earlier social media innovation. Originally these were primarily hosted on personal computers and users had to dial in through the host computer's modem. Online forums also played a large part in the evolution of the social web. Six Degrees was launched in 1997 and was the first modern social network. It allowed users to create a profile and to become friends with other users. It was Shut down in 2001. The emergence of Web 2.0 inaugurated a revolution in the social media innovations[6]. In Web 2.0 software applications are built upon the Web as opposed to upon the desktop. It is characterized by interactive nature and instant response. The earlier web solutions were almost static and allowed only one way communication. There was no feedback mechanism and provisions for interactions. The coming of Web 2.0 provided for instantaneous interactions between users and it also accommodated multiple interactions at any given time. Social medias sprouted and surpassed static web platforms within a short span of time.

Table 2: Mile stones in Social Media Development.

Sl. No.	*Year*	*Event*
1.	2002	LinkedIn launched
2.	2004	Facebook Launched
3.	2005	You Tube Launched
4.	2006	Twitter Launched
5.	2010	Instagram Launched
6.	2012	Face Book reaches One Billion Users
7.	2013	Twitter reaches One billion users
8.	2016	3.5 Billion Internet users,

(*Source:* Compiled from Measuring the Information Society Report 2016 (ITU, 2016)

Friendster was the first modern, general social network. Founded in 2002, Friendster is still a very active social network; with over 90 million registered users, it is popular in Asia. Hi5 (2003) is another major social network. The network currently claims 60 million active members supports. LinkedIn (2003) was one of the first mainstream social networks devoted to business. Myspace (2003) is another prominent player in the field. In 2006, it was rated as the most popular social network in the world. However, the comings of Face book in 2004 revolutionized the scenario. In 2008 Face book became the most popular social networking site, surpassing Myspace, and continues to grow. Orkut (2004) is another popular social network with 65 million users. YouTube was the first major video hosting and sharing site, launched in 2005. Users can upload videos up to 10 minutes long and share them through YouTube or by embedding them on other websites. With the advent of Twitter in 2006, status updates have become the new norm in social networking. The advent of What's app inaugurated a new era of social sharing in the web space. It makes intergroup communication cheap and easy.

Table 3: Social Media Usage Statistics as on 31-01-2017.

Sl. No.	*Particulars*	*Numbers*
1.	Facebook (Monthly Users)	1,100,000,000
2.	Twitter (Monthly Users)	310,000,000
3.	What's App (Monthly Users)	One Billion
4.	You Tube (Monthly Users)	120 Billion

(*Source*, Compiled from ITU (2016) and various internet sources)

Presently Twitter is in possession of 310,000,000 active monthly users. As on January 31, 2017, Face Book is used by 1,100,000,000 people monthly. The What's app monthly traffic has reached one billion people whereas You tube usage figures has crossed 120 billion per month. The figures clearly evidence that social media has a larger role in modern society.

Major state actors well acknowledge the importance of new social media all over the world[7]. Besides well laid policy documents many countries include constitutional provisions for the promotion of new social spaces. The importance of social media platforms is well acclaimed by the UN Human Development Report. It observes,

> In the 21st century's communication revolution, social networking sites have opened new and increasingly popular channels for social and

political participation. Social media are two-way and interactive, so people can collaborate and share information in efficient and effective ways. Social networking websites have become platforms for awareness raising, social mobilization, political discussion, and fundraising (World Bank 2012:340).

The new social media is becoming more integrated into people's lives and has shown its potential to alter political outcomes. It alters the pattern of democratic discourses and political orientations. Social media is now becoming a prominent communications tool rather than an IT application[8]. With the increasing spread of social media and mobile communication, the social networks of knowledge construction are becoming vastly bigger and quicker and less limited by space and time constraints. The basic characteristic of a media is its mass appeal and mass acceptance. At any point of time the media should be able to communicate with several people. Unlike traditional media, social media has a larger social context since it is targeted toward the public and deals mainly with social issues. In the case of traditional media its access to the public is limited by the subscription peripheries. They were also limited by issues like hierarchical structures, political linkages, business concerns, public scrutiny, cultural pressures etc. But the new social media enjoys several freedoms with respect to their organization and operations. They have the clear cover of anonymity and operational mechanism are simple enough to attract any one to own and operate a social media tool.

Human rights in digital society

The idea of social network suggests a map of specified ties, such as friendship, between the nodes. As such it provides interactive platform for discussion and communication. The hierarchical patterns of communications are replaced with horizontal patterns of collaborative interactions. New institutions and paradigms are created in tune with the cyber culture imposed and propagated by the new media. In the dominion of politics and democracy the new social media enhance participation capacities and reinforce political orientations. By the help of new tools new social spaces are created and existing ones widened. These new spaces are conducive for effective human right debates and solid public actions for human right protection.

Social media platforms offer a potential avenue for human right movements and actions. Social media exposes many human right violations and becomes a turbulent forum for Human right debates. Peripheral groups are acquiring avenues for democratic engagement and become competent actors in the system to raise their claims against the mighty restrictions of the state apparatus. The new social media is also complimented as market of new social capital, where social networks are created and social links are nurtured in an unprecedented manner and scope[9]. The development of new social capital in turn promotes public engagement and creates new civic spaces. These spaces are dominantly democratic and envisage a civic pattern of social culture. It is established that the new social media promotes citizen debates and engagements in an unprecedented scale and nature. Here comes the argument on human right platform.

The social media creates new awareness on human rights. There are possibilities to foster institutional mechanisms for protecting the human rights. Apart from revealing human rights violation in remote and inaccessible locations, the social media is capable of addressing everyday violence like domestic violence, political issues etc. A blog post, a face book sharing or a simple SMS can make a lot of changes. In this respect, social media enjoys a lot of freedom and immunity.

It is found that the internet and social media brings together individuals who do not otherwise engage in political or public life. There are many instances of public action which restrained political authoritarianism by the state or by international communities. The World Human Development Report 2016 very clearly attest this social media activism;

> On several occasions in recent years, large numbers of people have signed online petitions to draw the attention of policymakers to their opinions. In 2010, 2 million petitioners succeeded in banning politicians convicted of crimes from running for office in Brazil. In 2012, an online petition received 1.8 million signatures in support of the recognition of Palestine as a state by the United Nations. In 2014, 2.3 million people signed an online petition to oppose the eviction of the Maasai people from their ancestral lands by the Tanzanian government. Since 2010 the United Kingdom has provided the opportunity for citizens to petition Parliament on an issue by gathering 100,000 signatures. In 2003, online mobilization led protests in several countries against the war in Iraq. Over the past 10 years this trend has encompassed protests by civil society organizations and protests prompted by individuals who join over a specific issue and then disengage from political discourse. An important aspect of these protests is their geographic scope, sometimes spanning several cities and sometimes several countries. (Jahan 2016:40).

Human Rights beyond state

In a general sense the state is assumed to be a mechanism to protect and promote human rights. It makes laws and regulations and provide institutional mechanisms like human rights commissions to protect human rights. The international organizations also champion the case of human rights through various covenants and treaties. At the same time, institutional violations of human rights are less attended by the mechanisms and at times they are beyond the purview of public scrutiny. The state may have conventional excuses of sovereignty, security, defense and the like to shield institutional violators from legal mechanisms. With rapid proliferation of computer networks and popularization of social media, broad array of economic and political activities was channelized through the digital medium. This raised critical questions about the effectiveness of current framings of state authority. The distributive potentials of digital networks having been upheld, hierarchical state controls and authority were forced to democratize in a horizontal pattern. In this context, Coleman(2007) refers to de-regulation of the political state and further democratisation. A new public sphere is emerging in connected societies. The new public sphere is characterised with closer links and better communications. The net result is a continous public scrutiny of state power through social media. Political excess will be brought to light and the civil society may revolt against any authoritarian measures. From the 'Arab spring' to the 'occupy wall street' movement, there are numerous instances where the new media upheld democracy as the most essential ingredient for the establishment of a political environment that respect human rights.

A major characteristic of the new human rights movements imitated by social media is that accommodates different interests in society. People get increasingly connected and the connected world becomes increasingly socialized. For example, the anticorruption movement of Anna Hazare in India was highly promoted by new social media. A large number of IT professional youth joined the movement. It is observed that they were highly apolitical in political orientations and they moved for a political mission that initially was anti political. This was made possible with the social media intervention. The provision of technological means enable the new participants to derive new ways of existence and institutionalization, possibly free from larger state intervention. This new public sphere is ultimately a strong socialization tool and agency that promote freedom and democracy. The system itself is undergoing a transformation from democratic state to democratic society.

Social media are promising spaces of enhancing democracy and human rights and spaces of control at the same time. Freedom of expression and protection of privacy are assets compatible with the conditions of real time transnational participation in public debate, in the formation of cultural community and the integration of individual differences. These participatory social platforms might even break the rigid structures of undemocratic regimes. For some, this is a symptom of the revolutionary and liberating capacities of the social media and of their possibilities as multipliers, diffusors, and practitioners of human rights (Sarikakis and Rodriguez-Amat 2012:556).

The intervention of ICT positively influences the decision-making structure in any given society. Dominating majority loses the monopoly of information. Every citizen becomes empowered with information. Once the information becomes a common property, Human right violations are easily identified and disclosed. Consequently, people will organize themselves to protect their rights. This is well evidenced with the Philippine 'Smart Mob' of 2001. On January 17, 2001, during the impeachment trial of Philippine President Joseph Estrada, loyalists in the Philippine congress voted to set aside the key evidence against him. Less than two hours after the decision was announced, thousands of Filipinos, angry that their corrupt president might be left off the hook, converged in Manila. The protest was arranged, in part, by forwarded text messages reading, "GO 2EDSA, WEAR Blk". The crowd quickly swelled, and in the next few days, over a million-people arrived, choking traffic in Manila. It is estimated that Seven million messages were sent within a week. Despite the supportive attitude of the Congress the president was sent out of power within three days. (Shirky, 2011).

Many environmental movements were organised through social media initiative. In 2014 the platform Avaaz.org coordinated a gathering of more than 400,000 people in Manhattan — and hundreds of thousands more in other cities — for the "biggest climate march in history.

Arab Springs and the Human and the lessons

The Arab springs offers the best example for the role of social media and internet in promoting human rights (Thomas 2014). Generally Arab revolution is named after a set of public reactions against many oppressive regimes in the middle east. The earliest movement in this direction started in Tunisia on December 17,2010. Actually these revolutions were not the product of social media interventions. Social media helped activists to find each other and enabled their discussions and activities to become more visible. In Tunisia the revolution began, when a Tunisian police officer slapped and spat on a street peddler who had begged her not to confiscate his cart and produce. When Mohamed Bouazzi went to the police precinct to file a complaint he was ignored. Bouazzi returned an hour later, doused himself with gasoline and set himself aflame. In the days that followed, protesters stormed through towns throughout Tunisia. The army refused to take action against the demonstrators. On January 14, the ruler stepped down. Egyptian youth followed Tunisian events closely. Many Egyptian students, labor leaders and underground organizers had ties to labor and underground groups in Tunisia. On June 6, 2010, Khaled Said, a 28-year-old youth, died in police custody. Angry demonstrations had followed, and several youths created a Face book page "we are all Khaled Said." On January 11, the young Egyptian labor activist Asmaa Mahfouz distributed thousands of leaflets in Cairo's slums, and posted the now famous YouTube video exhorting Egyptians to join young women protesting "National Police Day," in Tahir Square on January 25. On February 11, the armed forces pushed the ruler out of power.

The Arab Springs were operated in the face of the most oppressive regimes and people were less organized prior to the revolution. But once the human right violations were shared through social media platforms the public sphere was revitalized. The activities of oppressive regime was also made public through the chatrooms and facebook comments and tweets. The phrase "tweeting the revolution" became commonplace as demonstrators detailed the minute to minute progress of protests to those elsewhere and abroad. According to a study by University of Washington, tweets about political change in Egypt rocketed from 2,300 a day to 230,000 on the day Mubarak resigned. Through the internet, revolutionary zeal spread from city to city, country to country, continent to continent. The global attention forced the governments to limit violence in suppressing the oppression. The role of social media in navigating the revolution is well outlined by an Amnesty document,

> Social media also gave common people the means to bring government abuse to light. In the absence of reporters, a new breed of "citizen journalists" armed with cell phone cameras self-published to websites such as Facebook, Twitter, YouTube, and WordPress. Khaled Said, a young Egyptian blogger, revealed police corruption in a video of officers distributing confiscated drugs among themselves. When he was beaten to death by two policemen as a result, the media claimed Khaled choked

> to death on a packet of drugs (Parker). However, a digital image of Khaled's bruised and bloody face was shared between thousands of mobile phones and on a 1.8 million member Facebook page made in his honor titled "We are all Khaled Said". "Suddenly, it's personal," said Egyptian activist Sally El-Bayoumi (Piachaud). Despite the government's efforts to cover up its injustices, the truth found an audience of millions through social media.
>
> (Tina Xu, The Arab Springs, and Social media, https://www.amnestyusa.org/pdfs/TinaXuEssay.pdf, Accessed on 12-03-2017)

The significance of Arab Springs lies not only in toppling down autocratic governments but also in organizing people. The social media was well used by the organizers to inform the public on human right issues and to initiate debates on the same[10]. This model was later replicated in the initiatives like 'occupy wall street' movement. Occupy Wall Street (OWS) was a protest movement that began on September 17, 2011, in New York City's Wall Street financial district, receiving global attention and spawning the movement against economic inequality worldwide[11]. The OWS movement was organized with the help of social media interactions. People from different part of the country joined the movement as social media spread the news immediately.

> At this juncture, the factor we can most certainly identify in explaining the spread of Occupy is the role of the Internet, social media, and other alternative media platforms. The title from earlier in this piece, "OWS Goes Viral," can be used to describe not just the police mace video but the broader nature of the movement's spread: indeed, occupy spread out of New York's Zuccotti Park much as the year's hottest YouTube video would. People with no previous relationship to any conscious "Left" found themselves clicking on Facebook posts and searching for updates on what had happened the night before. Many who did have prior left tendencies or affiliations were of course also hooked, and the suddenly rich, dense, and variegated online presence of Occupy enhanced the sense that something large and important was happening not just on- but also off-line, out there in the real world (Earle 2012:13).

Government initiatives to curb individual freedom and liberty is well opposed by large network of net based citizen groups. The government of US initiated a bill to regulate internet namely, Stop Online Piracy Act, in 2011. The act is supposed to bring strong regulations on internet copyright and allied fields. The bill was met with heavy opposition from the public and civil society. Wikipedia organized an online campaign against the Act and 162 million individuals signed the online petition[12].

Conclusion

Social media provides a potential avenue for new social movements and actions. The new social media is also complimented as a market of new social capital, where social networks are created and social links are nurtured in an unprecedented manner and scope. The development of new social capital in turn promotes public engagement and creates new civic spaces. These spaces are dominantly democratic and envisage a civic pattern of social culture. It is established that the new social media promotes citizen debates and engagements in an unprecedented scale and nature. It offers a big forum for human right activism. The global community can freely discuss human right issues and any violation can be fought globally. But on the other side critics are in legion. The first argument is that the democratic potentials of social media can be effective only if the society is democratic. An authoritarian society can become more authoritative via new technologies. The surveillance and monitoring potentials of the internet is widely used by democratic states also. There is increasing individualization and fragmentation of the mediated online world in the interests of the state in surveillance and security and in the interests of corporate in wealth creation. It is argued that new social media also reflect the power structure of the capitalist society and dances with the tunes of globalization. The privacy of the unsuspected actors in the forum is violated. The 'Big data' in possession of the operators make state monitoring and control of the individual more smooth and effective. There are many state-created issues like negative legislation, blocking and filtering. Social media debates are closely watched by the state and they try to impose strict controls[13]

The social media has initiated many revolutions. These revolutions were marked by the huge participation and the voluntary nature of those participations. There is also a trend to exempt conventional political actors from these movements. The depoliticization of a political movement has long term impacts including sustainability questions. The thumb revolutions are more easy and comfortable. But at the same time, it leaves lesser and non-durable political memories. The problem here is that the post-revolutionary structures may be fragile and less durable. In the debate on human rights also there is issues like sustainability and durability. The comfort of the thumb media need not be reflected in the real-time context.

The digital divide is another major concern. There are still many people who are yet to benefit from the connectivity revolution. Accessibility is still dominated by the privileged sections of society and the politics of peripheries is still a distant dream. Inexpensive and reliable access to the Internet is becoming essential to the development of capabilities in other areas, such as education, work and political participation. The biggest challenge is to make these benefits available to all people everywhere.

However, beyond these concerns social media provides for a new democratic culture, which accepts human rights as the foundation of any social structure. The growth of new technologies incorporates subalterns of modern society to the centre of political action. They are capable of creating new political spaces that stands for freedom and rights. Joseph (2012) observes,

> Presently, social media in its various forms has created an unprecedented global public space that vastly increases and amplifies the number of accessible voices and connections in all parts of the world. In the future, governments or other powerbrokers might seize control or compromise these platforms, and social media corporations might change their largely benign or even supportive attitude toward activism. For now, however, this digital communications Hydra provides a unique platform for millions of people to proclaim, in voices and actions heard around the world, that they are "as mad as hell and they aren't going to take it anymore." (Joseph 2012:188)

References

1. Anderson, Janna Quitney. 2010. *The Impact of the Internet on Institutions in the Future.* Washington D.C.: Pew Research Center.
2. Bedi, Kiran, Paraminder Jeet Singh, and Sandeep Srivastava. 2001. *Government@net; New Governance Opportunities for India.* New Delhi: Sage.
3. Bingham, Lisa Blomgren, Tina Nabatchi, and Rosemary O'Leary. 2005. "The New Governance: Practices and Processes for Stakeholder and Citizen Participation in the Work of Government." *Public Administration Review* 65 (5): 547-558.
4. Coleman, Stephen. 2007. "E-Democracy : The History and Future of an Idea." In *The Oxford Handbook of Information and Communication Technologies*, by Robin Mansell, Chrisanthi A Verrerou and Roger Silverstone, 362-382. New York: Oxford University Press.
5. Coleman, Stephen, and Jay G Blumer. 2009. *The Internet and Democratic Citizenship: Theory, Practice and Policy.* New York: Cambridge University Press.

6. Dunleavy, Patrick, Helen Margetts, Simon Bastow, and Jane Tinkler. 2005. "New Public Management Is Dead—Long Live Digital-Era Governance." *Journal of Public Administration Research and Theory* 16: 467–494.
7. Earle, Ethan . 2012. *A Brief History of Occupy Wall Street.* New York: Rosa Luxemburg Stiftung.
8. Hofheinz, Albrecht. 2011. "Nextopia? Beyond Revolution 2.0." *International Journal of Communication* 5: 1417–1434.
9. Howard, Philip N, Saiph Savage, Claudia Flores Saviaga, Carlos Toxtli, and Andres Monroy-Hemandez. 2016. "Social Media, Civic Engagement, and the Slacktivism Hypothesis: Lessons from Mexico's "El Bronco"." *Journal o f International Affairs* 70 (1): 55-73.
10. ITU. 2016. *Measuring the Information Society Report 2016.* Geneva: International Telecommunication Union.
11. Jahan, Selim . 2016. *Human Development for All-HumanDevelopment Report 2016.* New York: United Nations Development Programme.
12. Jeffrey, Robin, and Assa Doron. 2013. *Cell Phone Nation.* Gurgaon: Hachette India.
13. Joseph, Saraha. 2012. "Social Media, Political Change and Human Rights." *Boston College International and Comparative Law Review* 35 (1): 145-188.
14. Lane, Jan Erik. 2009. *State management.* New York: Routledge.
15. Sarikakis, Katharine, and Joan Ramon Rodriguez-Amat. 2012. "Human Rights Online or on the line? The Role of New (social) Media in Human Rights Protection." In *All Human Rights for All.*, by Nowak M Januszewski and Hofstätter T, 552-660. Vienna: Neuer Wissentschaftlicher Verlag.
16. Shirky, Clay. 2011. "The Political Power of Social Media Technology;The Public Sphere and Political Change." *Foreign Affairs* 90 (1): 28-41.
17. Thomas, Sabu. 2014. "Public Power and Technology: Evaluating the Role of Information and Communication Technology In Arab Springs." *Majalla Kairala* 3 (1): 148-154.
18. World Bank . 2012. *Human Development Report 2012.* Washington DC: World Bank.

Notes

1. In the strict sense the term ICT includes not only the digital or electronic means. It includes every communication tools. For example, UNESCO's use of the term refers to all forms of technology that are utilized to transmit, process, store, create, display, share or exchange information by electronic means. This broad definition of ICT includes radio, television, video, DVD, telephone (both fixed line and mobile phones), satellite systems, and computer. But in the present context the term ICT mainly targets digital technologies including computer, internet, mobile phone, and the like.
2. In 2012, only three countries, out of 193 UN Members (Central African Republic, Guinea and Libya) did not have a web presence (UN E-Government Survey, 2012:39). By 2016 these countries also created their official websites and all the

UN members are currently have web presence. The state of North Korea long relied on a total restriction of information to maintain control over its isolated citizenry. Later they shifted the policy and internet access was open to the public. However internet connectivity is still not permitted for foreign tourists. (Source N. Korea Cuts 3G Mobile Web Access for Foreign Visitors, http://www.voanews.com/a/north-korea-cuts-3g-mobile-web-for-foreign-visitors/1630236.html,Accessed on 12-05-2017).

3. According to the Human Development report 2016, presently 159 governments publish information online on finance, 151 on health, 146 on education, 132 on labour, 130 on the environment and 123 on social welfare (Jahan, 2016:110)
4. Global high-technology exports have more than doubled in the last 15 years, from $987 billion in 1999 to $2,147 billion in 2014.
5. The Organization for Economic Cooperation and Development (OECD) specifies three criteria for content to be classified as "user generated:" (1) it should be available on a publicly accessible website or on a social networking site that is available to a select group, (2) it entails a minimum amount of creative effort, and (3) it is created outside of professional routines and practices.
6. The term 'Web 2.0' was coined by Darcy DiNucci in 1999 in the article "Fragmented Future".
7. The United Nations (UN E-GovernanceSurvey-2012) also identifies social media as a potential boost for E-Governance. The report suggests, "For greater e-service take-up Governments need to make concerted efforts to exploit the full potential of social media to deliver messages and information services, promote awareness for greater citizen e-service take-up, and garner valuable user feedback and suggestions for service improvements. This implies that governments need to leverage social media for greater e-government service usage by citizens, including the poor, the elderly and other disadvantaged groups. As social media become widespread and mainstream, the strategic engagement of all groups in this new e-service usage channel becomes even more important. Governments should therefore strengthen their presence on existing social media sites and promote e-services, particularly those conducive to sustainable development, while also trying out new channels and sources of feedback, and new platforms and networks to bring together citizens and stakeholders. Thereby, governments can also share information about successful e-service take-up and utilization to further encourage citizens' usage of e-services. (UN E-Survey 2012:113).
8. The International Telecommunication Union Report (2016) observes, "While use of the Internet and online services is constantly expanding to new horizons, it is still mostly limited to communication with family and friends. Sending and receiving e-mails represents the most frequent activity in nearly all the 67 countries with household data on Internet use. While e-mailing is still increasing in many parts of the world, however, it is being complemented, and even replaced, by other forms of online communication through social media and instant messaging. In Turkey, for example, the proportion of Internet users stating that they frequently sent and received e-mails fell from 69 per cent in 2010 to 58 per cent in 2013. In 2013, 84 per cent of Turkish Internet users stated that they regularly participated in social media. In the Republic of Korea, more people

indicate that they participate in social media or frequently access chat sites, blogs, newsgroups, or online discussions than people indicating that they send and receive e-mails. In Europe, nine out of ten Internet users regularly send and receive e-mails, whereas two out of three participate in social media" (ITU 2016).

9. The crowd funding is one of the best examples of nurturing social relations. Crowdfunding allows individuals to contribute small amounts of money towards a philanthropic project that requires larger funds. Donors can fund local projects through civic crowdfunding or projects in other countries through charity crowdfunding. Spacehive, a civic crowdfunding platform in the United Kingdom, specializes in raising funds for small community projects such as improving a playground or renovating a school. It has raised nearly £5 million (more than $6 million) since its launch in 2011.

10. Wael Ghonim, Google's Middle East marketing director, and a participant of Arab revolution observes how the technologies fortifies the individuals against the fear of authority. The individual is allied with a network. He says, "Yet, nothing was happening...The reason everyone was silent was...the psychological barrier of fear... And that psychological barrier of fear has worked for so many years. And here comes the Internet. Technology. Blackberry. SMS. It's helping all of us to connect. Platforms like YouTube, Twitter, Face book were helping us a lot, because they basically gave us the impression that, "Wow — I'm not alone!" For detailed discussion see (Hofheinz, 2011).

11. The main issues raised by Occupy Wall Street were social and economic inequality, greed, corruption and the perceived undue influence of corporations on government—particularly from the financial services sector. The OWS slogan, "We are the 99%", refers to income inequality and wealth distribution in the U.S. between the wealthiest 1% and the rest of the population.

12. See Balaraman, *US Parliament Nettil Kurungunnu, (Malayalam),* Mathrubhumi, 25-01-2012, http://www.mathrubhumi.com/story.php? id=247287, Accessed on 25-01-2017.

13. The Commissioner for Human right, Council of Europe observes the scenario very vividly in a discussion paper, "We may think we are free and unobserved when we surf the Internet, chat with friends, send out tweets or upload video clips from our mobile phone. In practice, essentially everything we do or say or watch on the Internet is logged, and in principle available for analysis – unless we take elaborate precautions. If we do, that in itself is likely to flag us up to those watching. This allows repressive states to monitor and link activists, with a view to harassment, arrest and worse. Even in liberal democracies, this has led to the monitoring of peaceful activists" (Korff (2012), Social Media and Human Rights, Issue Discussion Paper, Council of Europe Commissioner for Human Rights, February 2012:13).

11

Human Rights and Cyber World

—Ashalekshmi B.S

The Internet has vast potential to increase the level and intensity of communication. Like other media, there are close linkages between the technology and human rights. Because of the relevance of the internet in all spheres of life, it touches on nearly all human rights. With an increasing number of people online there arises a growing expectation of rights and the protection of these rights. In that sense, it is more and more clear that there is a need for recognising existing human rights in cyberspace and on the Internet, and that these human rights are open to being violated by different entities in the cyber world, not necessarily just States but also private entities and internet providers.

Evolution of Information Technology and Human Rights

A core part of human rights is about communication and information, and a range of media theories address the connection between information, communication, news media and their political impacts. There are three great mediamorphoses in human communication: spoken language, written language, and the digital language. Spoken language led to social group formation, complex problem solving skills, and the development of 'broadcast' forms like storytelling and ritual performance, which in turn divided society into performers, gatekeepers, and audiences. Written language ushered in the development of portable documents, mechanical printing, and mass media. Early long-distance communication systems were based on postal and courier networks, and the corresponding concern by civil society was over the ability of governments to censor and prevent the transfer of mail. This was followed by the growth of telegraphy, telephony and radio, each of which evolved along different trajectories with respect to universality and communication rights in the international context. The rise of transnational telecommunications networks led to international standards bodies, formed around the deployment of postal services, telegraphy, telephony and radio, to resolve conflicts that they raised. It was in this context that the notions of universal service and freedom of transit for communications began to emerge. The Universal Postal Union (UPU) was established in1874 and helped shape concepts such as freedom of transit in the transfer of mail through third countries. The International Telegraph Union was founded in 1865, and universality was a stated goal from the outset. The ITU Convention of 1865, which was updated with the invention of the telephone in 1876, articulated support for the availability of telecommunication services for all citizens. Universality in this context was probably concerned more with practical matters such as interoperability, than with moral and ethical considerations. Radio was invented in 1895, followed by the formation of the International Radio-Telegraph Union (IRU) which addressed issues of spectrum allocation and non-interference. Radio was the first ICT to bring a broad range of citizens into its fold, and evolved into a public discourse medium. In 1934, the International Telegraph Union and the International Radio-Telegraph Union merged to form the International Telecommunications Union (ITU). In 1925, the US Communications Act mandated universal service for telephony in the US. The development of the United Nations and its Universal Declaration of Human Rights in the aftermath of World War II added a human rights context to these technological and regulatory developments. Another branch of human rights arose in the nineteenth century, in response to the consequences of the industrial revolution: economic, social, and cultural rights including the right to education, housing, health, employment, adequate income, and social security. Both these branches of human rights have converged into modern day concepts of rights and privileges.

Radio and television, as compared to print media, share several characteristics that have made them especially important in a communication rights context: use of their output is not dependent on literacy; they enable the broadcasting of information over large geographical areas; content creation barriers are high but access costs are lower. The Internet has changed this dynamic by reducing the costs of content creation, and making the reach of communications more global, instant and archived. Mobility has added the "anytime anywhere anydevice"dimension to the online ecosystem.

The relation between the Internet and most rights contained in the UDHR, starts from the right to non-discrimination in Internet access, to education, access to knowledge, online participation in public affairs and effective participation in Internet governance. The major rights of concern to the Internet, however, are freedom of expression and information, and the right to privacy and data protection.

The Right to Access to the Internet

The right to access to the Internet, which is the first right spelled out by the draft Charter is derived from the conclusion that all the Internet-related rights depend on having access to the Internet in the first place. This has also been recognised by different international bodies like the Council of Europe and the Joint Declaration on Freedom of Expression and the Internet by the four international Special Rapporteurs on freedom of expression. Still there is some debate whether the right to access should be considered a human right, because it is argued that access to a technology, to a tool, cannot be a human right. However, recent reports confirm access as a human right. There is less controversy about the fact that the denial of access to the Internet as such or to part of its content through blocking and filtering is a violation of human rights.

Accessing and transmitting information through the World Wide Web has become a significant part of contemporary lifestyles and entertainment, and has progressively developed into an awareness of a global community where the individual has the ability to connect socially and directly with other individuals without apparent political, social or racial borders. So called'second life' social experiences, have also reinforced the idea of cyberspace as a domain in which the individual may find, develop and exploit their own 'parallel reality'. Influential literature from almost four decades ago significantly altered the perception of cyberspace and the web and, together with an increased awareness of the right to access directly information and knowledge (also as a substitute for declared but not suffi ciently implemented human and social rights, to include the right to information), encouraged the perception of cyberspace as a 'global common'.

Freedom of Expression

In the last decades very few, if any, developments in information technologies have had such a revolutionary impact as the creation of the Internet has had on the freedom of opinion and expression. Unlike any other medium that communicates one way (newspapers, television and radio) the Internet represents a new way seen as being an interactive medium. The innovation lies in that intermediary platforms are created that facilitate participatory information sharing and where individuals play an active role in creating an aggregated content. Individuals are not only recipients of information, but also active producers of information. These platforms have a particular value in countries where there is no inde pendent media and where information is controlled by the government. The true innovation with Internet development lies in that information is being shared and that individuals can be part in expressing their right to freedom of expresion and opinion.

It is acknowledged, that some forms of freedom of expression can harm the rights of others. There is a difference between freedom of opinion and freedom of expression in that the former is seen as an absolute right from where no interference is permitted from society.19 Freedom of expressions on the other hand, is not absolute, and can in some cases be legitimately restricted under international human rights law, primarily in order to safeguard the rights of others. However, any limitation that a state is planning on the freedom of expression is a very sensitive matter.

Participation and Right to Equality

The challenge to public administration is not only the delivery of services but also addressing the full-fledged participation of all citizens, especially women. Addressing the gender dimensions of e-Governance poses an added set of challenges. Information and communications technology (ICT) is affected by and in turn affects the different opportunities that exist for men and women in relation to education, training and skills development, employment and working conditions, content development, and access to power structures and decision-making processes. ICT can be an effective tool for enhancing the provision of public service to citizens as well as for economic development, while promoting increased education and knowledge. However, women are vastly underrepresented in government, in business, in political and social institutions; they continue to access and use ICT to a much lesser extent than men. Men still hold most managerial positions in telecommunications companies and regulatory or policymaking bodies; regulatory decisions are usually made without any gender-impact analysis; and service licences are handled by private companies without due attention to equal opportunity policies.(UnitedNations,2005).

While access to ICT is fundamental, it is not sufficient by itself. The percentage of women's Internet usage does not correlate directly with a country's rate of Internet penetration. Unless specific, targeted gender goals and strategies are implemented in ICT projects, women would not have equal access or benefit to the same extent as men. If women are not directly targeted as beneficiaries of e-Governance, they will not be able to access information on government services, health and other issues which they need to support their livelihoods and well-being; nor will they be able to interact meaningfully with their Governments or participate in local governance forums and decision-making processes. Unless specific efforts are made to meet women's information needs, they will not find information that is relevant and useful. Encouraging and including the perspectives of women in policy design and implementation and ensuring that they receive the benefits of e-governance would enhance the prospects of addressing gender equality and the Millennium Development Goals. Conversely, these goals cannot be achieved without the inclusion of women.

Providing health services and information

E-Health services can contribute in situations where there is a lack of specialized staff, shortage of medical expertise (particularly in rural areas), limited access to medical education and scarce data on health-related issues. They also have the potential of helping women and men to understand their own health, including prevention and dealing with health concerns, through the packaging and dissemination of easy-to-understand health information in a variety of media. A study of 70 countries in Asia and sub-Saharan Africa found a significant correlation between telephone and television density and reducing malaria deaths. Telephones can help by providing connections to larger social networks and facilitating rapid diagnosis and treatment, while television can provide disease prevention awareness among the population, encourage people to adopt healthy behaviour and communicate risk mitigation actions(P. Mozumde and A. Marathe, 2007).

Right to Education

ICT-enabled education has great potential for increasing educational opportunities for women at all levels, in both formal and non-formal educational environments. ICT can also expand access to training programmes, from basic online courses on leadership, health, and The growing prevalence of computers in primary schools and use of ITapplications offer excellent opportunities to participate in social networks, develop advanced ICT skills and produce and share content out of their own experience.

To comprehend the current trends and the possibility of new threats to human rights protection, it is essential to examine the application of human rights in the digital age. As a result of development, the ambit of human rights law has expanded rapidly due to the influence of digitalization in the late 20th century. Nowadays, the applications of the Internet along with the many novelties to peoples′ interaction challenge the traditional notion of human rights law. The interaction between digital technology and human rights makes it extremely difficult to define human rights exhaustively in the context of cyberspace. Therefore, the dark side of cyberspace needs to be addressed because, for instance, cyber exploitation including virtual child pornography, liability and censorship issues together with privacy and surveillance problems create a tension relevant to both individuals and to the future of human rights law in general.

Digital Surveilance

Ware witnessng camera as the unblinking, unforgiving eye in our ICT environment. Facial, pattern and number recognition using digital technology is being deployed increasingly to detect socially undesirable behaviour. Public surveillance using Closed Circuit Television (CCTV) is becoming pervasive despite the absence of empirical evidence on the effectiveness of its use as a means of crime prevention. Klang argues that it is a matter of human choice as to which individuals or groups receive the greatest attention because of the need to select from the huge quantities of data that are being gathered. The provisions of European Convention on Human Rights, Article 8, implies that surveillance can be intrusive because of its potential for error, function creep, privacy invasion.

Cyber Exploitation and Virtual Pornography

The sexual exploitation of woman and children is a global human rights crisis that is being escalated by the use of new technologies. This can be interpreted to mean exploitation that is facilitated by the use of information and communication technologies (ICTs). The Internet, for example, offers an entirely new kind of advantage to both individuals and the whole sex industry to market, find and oppress woman. Hughes argues that digital media, such as newsgroups, websites and chatrooms can all be used for exploitation purposes as they serve as the perfect platform for this kind of criminal activity.It is uncertain how the issue of cyber exploitation should be addressed or who actually profits the most, but one thing is obvious; something needs to be done because the amount of ICTs keeps growing along with the new applications.

Another form of violation to human rights is child pornography that nowadays takes place both in real life and in cyberspace. Today the majority of consumption and production happens online as ICT has grown to be the most popular medium of distribution. Reasons for this are low costs if any, easiness and the ability to act anonymously. Since the mid-1990s, the whole child pornography industry has changed dramatically due to the development of digital interaction. A completely new kind of subculture has emerged as pedophiles have began to group up and share their fantasies online. One of the most repulsing incidents was the Orchid Club, exposed in California in May 1996.The Orchid Club was discovered when the police arrested one of the members on a charge of child sexual abuse. Involving individuals from countries as far afield as Finland, Australia, the United Kingdom and Canada, the Orchid Club is widely considered the first prosecuted case in which pictures of a child being molested were transmitted in real time using video conferencing software. Another issue is the so called morphed images (i.e. pseudo-photographs), created by the modern day software. They lack the real-life victim but amount to a certain degree of child pornography.

Defamation

With the help of global medium like the Internet, for example, the message can be made available for a larger audience at greater speed but also with less scrutiny and quality control. The Internet can be used simultaneously to provide passive information and to agitate active discussion. Chat-rooms, electronic bulletin boards, personal blogs, e-mails and virtual worlds all impose dangers to individuals and their reputation. In order to pursue someone for defamation there have to be both publication or communication and injurious statement present. Sometimes, it may be difficult to trace the original writer and the attention turns to the party actually distributing the message

Cyber Censorship and Digital Surveillance

One of the most fundamental principles to human rights law is the freedom to receive and communicate information. In the context of the digital age, the doctrine of free marketplace of ideas, however, is under pressure when technology is being used to filter information akin to censorship. For example, since the adoption of the European Union's 1997 Action Plan on Promoting Safe Use of the Internet, the EU has invested in many filtering projects such as NETprotect I and II projects, ICRAsafe project and the PRINCIP program. Another good example is the Safer

Internet Programme49 established in 1999 and later on extended to last till year 2008. The purpose of this program was to eliminate harmful, racist and illegal contents on the Internet by creating a standardized rating system. Firewalls, proxy servers, routers, other technology and self censorship are being used to block and filter certain kind of information as governments seek to observe the information on the Internet. The global surveillance methods may differ from mere controlling techniques (i.e. content analysis) to a total ban on access to a particular Web site, for example (i.e. blocking). In the eyes of the human rights law the blocking technique is a problematic issue because it may lead to information distortion and lack of transparency.

Access to information is also regulated on national level according to political agendas and on local level such as in cyber cafes etc. The former is being used in Syria where access to majority of the Israeli websites is blocked and the latter in many developing countries where the vast majority of people do not own personal computers. As mentioned above, the Internet indeed is not a completely *laissez-faire* free market as the global surveillance challenges global politics, civil society anddemocratic values.

Employee Surveillance Informational and communications technology has also made it possible for employers to monitor their employees by overseeing their telephone calls, e-mails or Internet use, for example. Sometimes this kind of surveillance may occur without the employee's knowledge and hence human rights such as right to privacy or right to private life are undermined. There have also been cases of employees fired by organizations for their social media activities that have included criticisms of either supervisors or the workplace. It seems that the human rights law will encounter numerous challenges as the digital age continues to expand even deeper into our lives.

There is an increasing apprehension of the potential that ICT offers for human development, despite the diverse kinds of human rights issues on cyber space. . In the future, newer, as-of-yet unknown varieties of ICTs may come along and offer currently incredible possibilities for the developing world. It is the need of the hour that a common International Rule of Law needs to get framed in order to tackle the human rights issues on cyber space if it is considered under 'global commons'.

Reference

Froomkin, Michael, 'Habermas@Discourse. Net: Toward a Critical Theory of Cyberspace' (2003) 116 *Harvard Law Review*.

Anandarajan, M., Simmer, C. A., & D'Ovidio, R. (2011). Exploring the underlying structure of personal web usage in the workplace. Cyberpsychology, Behavior, and Social Networking, 14(10), 577-583.

Martin, K., & Freeman, R. (2003). Some Problems with Employee Monitoring. Journal of Business Ethics, 43(4), 353-361.

Watson, A. M., Thompson, L. F., Rudolph, J. V., Whelan, T. J., Behrend, T. S., & Gissel, A. L. (2013). When big brother is watching: Goal orientation shapes reactions to electronic monitoring during online training. Journal of Applied Psychology, 98(4), 642-657. doi: 10.1037/a0032002

Gurumurthy, op. cit., 2006, p. 123. 34 E. Lallana, Government and eDemocracy (Washington, D.C., World Bank, 2007); visit also http://www.mgovworld.org/resources/m-government-and-e-democracy.

United Nations Department of Economic and Social Affairs, IPU and the Global Centre for ICT in Parliament, World e-Parliament Report 2008, New York, 2008 (ST/ESA/PAD/SER.E/124). Available from http://www.ictparliament.org/index.php?option=com_contact&task=view&contact_id=3&Itemid =1086.

P. Mozumde and A. Marathe, "Role of information and communication networks in malaria survival", in Malaria Journal (2007), vol. 6, p. 136; see also http://www.malariajournal.com/ content/6/1/136.)

Chatterjee, B, "Pixels, Pimps and Prostitues: Human Rights and The Cyber-Sex Trade Deibert, Ronald J., Crete-Nishihata, Masashi, 'Global Governance and the Spread of Cyberspace Controls' (2012) 18 *Global Governance.* http://citizenlab.org/cybernorms2012/governance.pdf

K. Acharya, "Flaws in Bhoomi, India's model e-governance project" (Pune, India, 2003). Available from http://archive.apnic.net/mailing-lists/s-asia-it/archive/2003/08/msg00027.html; Rahul De', "The impact of Indian E-Government initiatives: issues of poverty and vulnerability reduction and conflict". In Regional Development Dialogue, vol. 27, No. 2, 2006, pp. 88-100. http://www.uncrd.or.jp/pub/rdd/rdd27_2/pdf.

Klang, M & Murray, A, "Human Rights in the Digital Age" (2005), chapter 2, p. 15.

Lane III, F. S. (2003). The naked employee: How technology is compromising workplace privacy. AMACOM, division of American Management Association. NY, NY. pdf

Pekka Kijanen, (2008) New Generation for Human Rights in Cyberspace

Robin Mansell, (2009) Introduction - human rights and equity in cyberspace, LSE Research Onlne, London School of Economics and Political Science

United Nations, Department of Economic and Social Affairs, Division for the Advancement of Women, Gender Equality and Empowerment of Women through ICT (New York, 2005). Available from www.un.org/womenwatch/daw/public/2000-09.05-ict-e.pdf.)

Wolfgang Benedek, Madanmohan Rao Internet Handbook; Bangalore, India.

12

Between Industrial Development and Right to Life: The Struggle against Nitta Gelatine in Kathikudam, Kerala

— **Shaji Varkey**

Introduction

The narrative of modernity has been constructed in independent India through a process of urbanization and industrialization. The urban industrial imagination so deeply ingrained in the minds of people, was pitted against a rural agricultural structure. The elite consensus in favour of industries has eventually become the reigning ideology of the state. Slogans like industrialise or perish' (Iyer, 2007), as against a weak 'industrialise and perish' (Natraj, Misra and Kapoor, 2005) gained ascendancy across India and states were competing with each other for their share of the cake. As industrialization does not happen automatically, it has to be brought in, and the price to be paid for it is huge. The privileged child of industry received everything on a platter while its underprivileged sibling remained in poverty and perpetual misery. The state liberally provided what industries asked for; land, electricity, water, raw materials, credit, tax concessions, tariff protection etc. the latter has expanded phenomenally. Industries are notorious for violation of laws but the system always wanted to see that the production should never stop. Industries have a legal and moral obligation to the society, particularly in the aftermath of the passing of Air Act, Water Act and the Environment Protection Act. The various judicial pronouncements asserting that right to life is not mere animal existence gained wider currency thanks to civil society activism and democratisation of the judicial process.

Aphorism like 'polluter pays principle' and 'precautionary principle' have been invoked to point out the environmental wrongdoings of industries (Abraham, 1999).

1. Industries located in environmentally sensitive areas or close to water bodies are prone to causing more harm to the community. The dominant thought in Kerala has been that the state, being placed in an industrially disadvantaged position, necessarily has to move an extra mile to invite industries to Kerala. The Gwalior Rayon's case was illustrative as the first government of Kerala provided raw materials (reed and bamboo) for almost free (Seethi, 2000). The company had to pack up finally due to a sustained campaign against pollution. The pollution of the river Periyar due to the existence of over 100 red category industries has earned the ignominious title of 'toxic hotspot' (world rank 35) by Greenpeace International in 2003[1] The Periyar Malineekarana Viruddha Samithi has been sphere heading a campaign against the dirty industries in the area (Dwivedi, G.2011).

About Nitta Gelatin company

The Nitta Gelatin India Limited (NGIL) was established in 1975 at Kadukutty panchayat in Thrissur District. It is on the banks of Chalakkudi River. Until June 2008 it was known as Kerala Chemicals and Proteins Limited. The main products from the company are gelatin, collagen, peptide ossein and di-calcium phosphate. The change of name occurred when majority of the shares were bought up by the Japanese partner in 2008. Production of ossein from animal bones through a chemical process is done in Kathikudam. Water and hydrochloric acid are used in the production of ossein. Raw bones, several months old are brought from north India for the production of ossein. Earlier, the plant was using 18 tonnes of animal bones but the amount has increased to 127 tonnes/day in 2013, of which 7% is composed of rotten meat, bone sinew, excreta of rodents and microorganisms. This is converted into pet food. The rest of the substance (120 tonnes) undergoes chemical treatment for three days. At the end, protein and calcium and other inorganic substances are separated. Inorganic substances are mixed with calcium carbonate to produce di-calcium phosphate. This is an ingredient in the production of chicken feed. Half of the protein compound, known as ossein is exported to Japan and the other half is sent to the gelatin unit in Kakkanad. The company was drawing 20 million litres of water per day from Chalakkudi River without any sanction from any authority. An equal amount of untreated effluents was discharged into the river without undertaking any treatment. Out of the 89 tonnes of solid waste generated, 30 tonnes is discharged into the river. V.T Padmanabahan and Joseph Makkolikkal had estimated the amount of heavy metals discharged by the company as 20 kg of Cadmium and 2000 kg Lead annually. This is mostly present in solid waste and DCP[2].

The Supreme Court Monitoring Committee that came into being in 2006 has classified the NGIL waste as Hazardous Waste. The company produces 8.77 mt. ossein, 4.30 mt. limed ossein and 41.84 mt. of di-calcium phosphate per day. Process recovery generates dry bone meal of 2.4 mt sinews 2.5 mt, wet bone meal 2.25 mt. and animal fat 1000 kg per day.

Sources of industrial waste

The industrial waste in Kathikudam chiefly comes from three plants:

1. From ossein plant: this includes acidic water, grease, traces of oil, traces of flesh and sinew and other chemicals.
2. From limed ossein plant: water containing calcium carbonate.
3. From di-calcium phosphate plant: water containing large quantities of chloride.

   The *Jananeethi* Report, prepared by the fact finding team of scientists and social activists, found that the company compound was raised considerably by filling the land with sludge. To cover up the crime, the surface was covered with carpet grass. The huge deposit of sludge in the company compound has resulted in the leaching of the hazardous materials into nearby wells, paddy lands and water bodies[3].

   The unauthorized extraction of water by the company was unprecedented. The company had established its own pumping station on the bank of the Chalakkudi River. Two 60 hp. motors were installed that pump up water 24x7. The company does it without any permission.

Beginning of the agitation

The first visible protest against the company was made by Kannambalath Ayyappan Nair, a worker from public sector fertilizer company, FACT. His protest was mainly by way of memoranda submitted to various government authorities[4]. In 1982 T.D. Devassy, a resident near the company complained that the water he was using at home was polluted by the company and the latter should make alternative arrangements.

The company started paying Rs.300 a month to Devassy for buying water. In the same way another resident T.A. Xavier was given Rs.150 a month. On the basis of complaints from residents on the south of the company, a common tap was set up in 1984 to provide water[5].

In 1992 company inducted 50 new employees and increased production from the full capacity of 72 tonnes to over 150 tonnes. Naturally, the disposal of sledge became a new issue. The company started disposing the sledge in the laterite mining pits in its own compound. Some of the pits were 5-6 metres deep. After each layer of sludge, a layer of soil was spread over it. Anti pollution agitation against the company was intensified during 1995-96 when the waste thus disposed leached into nearby wells rendering the water unfit for domestic use.

Waste treatment during the initial years was crude. The plant is situated at an elevation. Paddy fields were located on two sides of the plant at a lower elevation. The company had strengthened the outer boundary wall and treatment tanks were built close to it. The water accumulated in the treatment tanks overflows into Karakkathodu, a nearby stream that eventually reaches Chalakudi River.

The one man fight by Shaju Joseph

The one-man fight against the plant by Shaju Joseph during 1995-96 is a significant epoch in the agitations against the company. He tried to raise the awareness about the waste and its toxic impact on human beings and the environment. He prepared a number of memoranda and sought official intervention from various government agencies. He even sought the support of community leadership of SNDP and NSS. He had printed and distributed about 15 different notices during 1995-96 period. Very few bureaucrats, politicians and local people had supported his ventures. According to Shaju Joseph "not even 10 people were available for the agitation. P.C. Gopi, Hamzakutty, Jalal, Joji and agricultural officer Sankaran were helping the agitation. They too were not consistently supporting the agitation. Due to local political and family pressures, none of them turned up for activities for more than twice". According to M T Ramesh, a resident of Kathikudam, who involved in the struggle, the public participation was so low "as people were afraid of the consequences"[6]. Shaju Joseph was critical of the local political leadership, including Congress and CPM. For Shaju, the company management was playing a strategic role whenever an agitation occurred. The company would incite workers to act against the struggle by saying that agitations would result in the closure of the plant. The Swathantra

Thozhilali Union, a breakaway group from INTUC was active in sabotaging agitations against the company.

Building up of agitation

A new anti-pollution front emerged in 2003 known as KPCL Malineekarana Viruddha Samithi (KPCL Anti-Pollution Action Council). It was formed on March 30[7]. The Samithi had elected K.K. Chandran as Convenor and E. Achuthan as Chairman. Majority of the members were from CPM. The Samithi had a short life as the Kadukutty Local Committee of the CPM intervened and asked the Samithi to stop its agitation activities. "Such opportunistic stance by political leaders has resulted in serious loss of credibility, even for genuine people engaged in agitation against the company. When they approached people to gather support, the former suspected it as an effort at extracting money from the management"[8].

Protests against the plant assumed a new dimension in 2008 when M.C. Gopi, T.T. Chandrasekharan, Binoy and Vipin, all youth from Kadukutty Panchayat had campaigned for starting a fresh fight against the company. The campaign ended with formation of KCPL Action Council on 23 March. Jayan Joseph Pattathu was elected as Chairman and Appu Kuttippad as General Convenor[9]. When the company had changed its name into NGIL in April 2008, the name of the action council was changed into NGIL Action Council. The Action Council has initiated several actions against the company. Finally an agreement was reached between the management and the Action Council on November 11, 2008. Under this, the company agreed not to discharge untreated effluents into the river and the solid wastes should not be sent out without proper records. The Action Council remained active for nearly 2.5 years since its formation in March 23, 2008. During this period the Action Council had grown into strength and gained acceptability. After the exit of Gopi and Chandrasekharan, the leadership came into the hands of Anil Kumar.

Effluent pipe burst

Another incident that provoked the local people was the pipe burst occurred on July 20, 2009. The company had laid an effluent discharge pipe made of iron two metres deep in the ground from the plant to Chalakkudi river. The distance of the pipe is about one kilometer. Corrosion of the metallic pipe had occurred at several points leading to waste spillage along the way to the river. People on various occasions in the past had complained about leakages on the pipe, but the management was not very keen on repairing it. As the waste water started accumulating in the nearby paddy lands and low lying areas, protest mounted. The Action Council had staged a protest in front of the plant. Realising the gravity of the situation, the Kadukutty Panchayat had suspended the licence given to NGIL. A free medical camp was organised jointly by Solidarity and Action Council on July 26, 2009 at Kathikudam L P School. It was found that out of 250 people who had attended, 14 were suffering from cancer[10]. According to Mirzad, a district committee member of Solidarity, the camp was able to create an ant-factory feeling among people[11].

Role of the village Panchayat

The Kerala Panchayat Raj Act says that a factory has to obtain licence from the local body to function within its jurisdiction and if the same is found to be "offensive or dangerous to human life or health" the latter can stop its function. According to Clause 232 of the Kerala Panchayat Raj Act "the village panchayat may notify that no place in the Panchayat area shall be used for any of the purposes specified in the rules made in this behalf being purposes which in the opinion of Government, are likely to be offensive or dangerous to human life or health or property, without a license issued by the 178(Secretary) and except in accordance with the conditions specified in such licence". Clause 233A (1) reads: "Where any factory, workshop, workplace or machinery causes, in the opinion of the village panchayat nuisance by reason of a particular kind of fuel being employed or by reason or the noise or vibration created, or effluent discharged or by reason of noxious odour, smoke or dust omitted, the secretary may direct the person in charge of such factory, workshop, workplace or machinery for the abatement of such nuisance within a reasonable time to be specified for that purpose". Clause 3 deals with the powers of Panchayat Secretary: "Where there has been wilful default in carrying out a direction given under subsection (1) or where in the existing circumstances the abatement of nuisance is found impracticable, the secretary may prohibit the working of the factory workshop, workplace or machinery till such time the person concerned takes necessary steps to the satisfaction of the secretary for the abatement of the nuisance"[12].

The goodwill from the Kadukutty Panchayat to NGIL vanished when the latter started polluting the environment and the people turning against the company for relief. The company's drive for enhanced production and profit at the expense of peoples health and environmental security, has created a wedge between the two. During 2009-2010, the Panchayat refused to renew the license. There are 32 residential houses situated within a radius of 100 meters from the company and certain houses are situated even closer by 80 metres from the location of the company. Therefore, considering the larger public interest, license was not renewed. When it was challenged in W.P.20891 of 2009, the High Court granted an interim order and directed to decide the question on the pollution by the Pollution Control Board.

During 2011 to 2016 the Panchayat refused to renew the licence. On the strength of the consent from PCB, the High Court periodically granted permission to the factory to function. The application filed by the company for issuance of sanitation certificate was rejected by the Health Inspector. The sludge accumulating in the premises of the company give out a nauseating smell causing suffocation to the local people within the area of 1 km. As the company has multiplied its production, new constructions and installations became necessary. This was done without the consent of the Panchayat. The Secretary on inspection found that buildings with a plinth are of about 33,000 square feet were constructed without building permit and machines with 4593 HP as against the sanctioned HP of 120 were installed.

Incident at the biogas plant

In another incident of pollution, the wall of biogas plant caved in on 1, November 2011. This has resulted in the spread of pollutants in the factory and consequent hospitalisation of 11 workers. After this incident the plant was temporarily closed. On 3 November, the workers unions in the plant had organised a joint demonstration. While inaugurating the demonstration, V.D. Satheesan MLA said that at no cost the company would be closed. P.M. Francis, a CITU leader said that if the company is closed, the massive collection of bones kept in the company premises would rot. This would result in a situation where no one could live. On 9th November a march was organised by the CPI(M) Kadukutty Local Committee towards the company demanding an end to mismanagement and also to restart the operation of the company after removing the waste completely[13]. A meeting was called at Collector's chamber on 10 November to discuss the issue. The Collector had ordered the closure of the plant till pollution issues are solved. The meeting was attended by T.N. Prathapan, B.D. Devassy, representatives from the management's side. The plant remained closed for a month. A strong opinion came up that the unauthorised pipe that the company laid for waste discharge be removed. Anil Kumar however, had a different opinion on this. He said that since the Chief Minister was calling a meeting and that there was no need for a hasty step at this point[14].

A discussion was held in the presence of Chief Minister on December 10, 2011. Industries Minister P.K. Kunhalikkutty, V.D. Satheesan MLA, B.D. Devassy MLA, Block Panchayat President Finso Thankachan, company representatives, Prof. Kusumam Joseph, Fr.George Pulikuthiyil, Jeyam Pankajakshan and M. Mohandas (all Action Council representatives) were in attendance. T.N. Prathapan did not attend. V.D. Satheesan was in favour of the company. Chief Minister and Industries Minister had adopted the stand that the company should be opened. Panchayat and Action Council representatives staged a walk out. It was decided to restart production at the company.

The appointment of Lakshmikutty Committee

From June 1997 onwards the Pollution Control Board had received several complaints from local residences against the company for causing water pollution and foul smell. Based on the complaints filed by the Action Council, the Government appointed an Expert Committee to study and report the alleged pollution from the company. As per the Industries Department order dated 27.01.2011, the Government appointed 8 member Expert Committee headed by Dr.Lakshmikutty, Head of the Department of Chemical Engineering, Government Engineering College, Thrissur. The Expert Committee submitted a report dated 03.11.2011. The recommendations were: 1. Reduce water consumption by using appropriate technology and water recycling method; 2. Construction of new biogas plant; 3. Improve the efficiency of DCP bag filters by installing additional bag filters; 4. Stoppage of semi-dried solid waste transportation to outside; 5. Execution of the directives from the PCB and complete adherence to pollution control norms; 6. Prevention of order from the company using modern technology; 7. Take sincere steps for the benefit and upbringing of local people and there by achieve their goodwill; 8. Formation of green belt along the company boundary; 9. Prevention of odour related pollution in the area; 10. Consider continuous monitoring system for assessing the smell in the surrounding; 11. Formation of monitoring committee comprising local body members, trade union members, management and health department ;12. Take steps to remove the apprehensions regarding outlet water discharge system; 13. Cleaning of Chalakudy river to remove the sediments from the river bed[15]. The Government directed the company to implement these recommendations from November[16]. At the meeting convened by the Chief Minister of Kerala on 7.12.2011 it was decided to strictly implement the 13 recommendations given by the Expert Committee. In addition to the above, three more items were included in this meeting as follows: 1. provide delay pond for treated effluent; 2. provide bag filters to reduce suspended matter and 3. enclose the crushed bone unloading area for reducing the smell.[17]

Kathikudam calling (Call of Kathikudam)

The 2013 agitation against the company started when large scale fish kills were noticed in the Chalakkudi river on May 29, 30 and June 1. This phenomenon was found for about 10 kms downstream from the point where effluent pipe empties into the river[18]. Premkumar, a resident of Moozhikulam was mainly responsible for the protests during this period. A meeting was held at Annamanada where a new body for protest was formed. It was known as *Kathikudam Samrakshana Samithi* (Kathikudam Protection Council). It included members of the Action Council as well. The purpose behind the formation of the new organisation was to include new entrants and to facilitate the re-entry of those who had left the struggle earlier[19]. The Samarasamithi elected T.R. Premkumar as Chairman and K.M. Anil Kumar as Convenor. At the meeting held at 'Moozhikulam Salai' an NGO for organic farming, the nitty gritty of 'Kathikudam calling', was worked out. According to Premkumar, a schedule of action for the next 30 days was prepared at the Moozhikulam meeting.

The protest started by raising black flags all over the Panchayat. From June 14, the Kathikudam Samara Samithi started hunger strike in front of the company. Every day one activist would observe hunger strike. From early June, activists of the Youth Dialogue had landed in Kathikudam and gave active support to the struggle. All online campaigns for the agitation were done by Youth Dialogue. The face book page 'Kathikudam Vilikkunnu (call of Kathikudam) was managed by the Youth Dialogue. This campaign had a positive impact among the public in Kerala. Several people had visited the *pandal* (venue) and declared their solidarity.

The NGIL was functioning on the basis of a High Court order as the Panchayat had stopped issuing license for its function. The High Court order permitted the company to function up to 30 June. The Samara Samithi had raised a new demand. The people, by exercising their power (*janaadhikaram*), would forcibly remove the unauthorized effluent pipe if it was not removed by the latter on their own[20]. When agitations started on the basis of this demand, the administration panicked. The collector had called a meeting on June 30 which was attended by B.D. Devassy, T.N. Prathapan, P.C.B. Engineer, Labour Union leaders and members of the Samithi. When collector mooted the idea of closure, all political parties had opposed it. It was decided to appoint a committee to study the pollution issue. The duration of the committee was 20 days. It consisted of District Collector and PCB members. On the basis of the discussion, Samithi suspended its agitation till 20 July 2013. Nothing happened in between this period. The company did nothing to improve the situation. On the expiry of the committee's period on 20 July, the Samithi had decided to remove the pipe. However due to outside political pressure this decision was deferred.

The Action against the company

The July 21 agitation against the company was historic. The decision of the Samithi was to protest against the company and to enforce a blockade at the company gate till the plant was closed. As scheduled, the protesters marched from the company gate to the effluent pipe. The protests passed off peacefully in the forenoon. T N Prathpan's inaugural speech had a dampening effect on the activists and social workers gathered from different parts of Kerala. He said that the agitation was in no way against the company. The objective was not to close down the plant but to stop pollution[21].

The police resorted to lathi charge in the evening when protesters refused to disperse. Chasing the people, the police ransacked the houses and destroyed household goods. The doors of houses were broke open and men folk were beaten and abused. Several women and children were injured in the police action. This received widespread condemnation across Kerala as the police brutality was directed against a crowd agitating peacefully. The company was closed for two days, apparently aimed at blunting the edge of the protest.

The Chief Minister called a meeting wherein the Industries Minister, B.D. Devassy, T.N. Prathapan, V.D. Satheesan (all MLAs), CPM leaders and representatives of trade unions, Panchayat, Samithi and company management were in attendance. The discussion ended in failure. The Samithi and panchayat stood for the closure of the factory while others opposed. The latter staged a walk out. The Samithi decided to impose blockade against the company from next day onwards. The protest had a poor start as there were hardly any protesters around in the morning. It was decided at the general body meeting held on 24th July that five protestors should observe fast on a daily basis and court arrest. After two days the arrested people were not granted bail. Ayesha B, an activist who courted arrest said that they were prepared to go to any extent for the cause[22]. The blockade lasted only for 15 days.

According to Premkumar efforts were made to democratise the movement. Every day a *Janakeeya sabha* (peoples forum) was convened where the course of the agitation and finance were discussed. According to Premkumar, another group did not tolerate this democratic structure. They became a 'conspiracy' group. T Chandrasekharan alleged that this group had collected funds without giving proper receipts from people during 2009 when Gopi and Chandrasekharan were raising funds for a new campaign[23]. The *Jankeeya Sabha* according to Prem Kumar had good participation. Even women and children were attending it.

LDF agitation against the company

Agitations against the company once again flared up when the pollutants escaped through the manhole and spread in the nearby paddy field on September 19, 2013. This time the CPI (M) had put up resistance against the company by forming a Samara Samithi of its own. The meeting was organised at Kathikudam U.P. School on September 21. It was inaugurated by A.C. Moideen, the CPM District Secretary, K.K. Nazeer was elected as the Chairman and T.V. Suresh as the Convenor of the Samara Samithi. Apart from the Chairman, the LDF Samithi had three Vice Chairmen, one Convenor, two General Conveners and an Executive Committee. On emergency situations, decisions were taken by convening the Executive Committee[24].

The CPM and DYFI were behind the formation of the Samara Samithi. Except CPI, no constituent units of the LDF had any presence in the panchayat. Action Council was excluded from the agitation. T.V. Suresh Kumar had some reasons for it. "We don't agree to their stand. They don't want to see that the agitation is ended. They wanted to live with it. They would not have an address if the protest ended now". T.R. Prem Kumar, who broke away from the Action Council shares an almost similar opinion. "Protest for them is a means of livelihood. Now I believe so. If otherwise, the protest would have succeeded long back. They want to see that the agitation continues like this. This gives images like 'leader of the popular protest'. The security it provides and the media attention it provides"[25]. The Samithi started its agitation on 22 September independently of the existing organisation. Initially they pitched their tent at the sight of pollution but later shifted the site in front of the company. According to *Keraleeyam*, the CPM had initially demanded the closure of the company, but later on, scaled down the demand to elimination of pollution[26]. According to L.C. Secretary, C.D. Paul and T.V. Suresh Kumar, the CPM Samithi was not in favour of closing the company. "Agitation by the left is issue-based. Action Council from the very beginning was demanding for the stoppage of production or closure of the company. LDF does not agree to this" said C.D. Paul.

On October 6, 2013, V.S. Achutanandan, the Opposition Leader had visited Kathikudam. What he witnessed was two protest sites in front of the company almost for the same cause. Two groups had made conflicting claims on the issue. According to Action Council Leader Anil Kumar, Achutanandan visited Kathikudam on their invitation. Seeing the danger, the LDF had organised a programme and invited him. C.D. Paul contracted this. He said "we invited Achutanandan, we organised a hunger strike on that same day. When Achutanandan came, C.R. Neelakantan (a prominent environmental activist from the Action Council side) and others wanted him to be taken to their protest *pandal.* He went there, wished them, returned to our pandal and spoke"[27].T.R. Premkumar had a different opinion with Achutanandan. "He took us for a ride. He promised to visit Kathikudam four times. He used to visit places where he can reap political mileage, or where his advisors suggest him to go. He would not get any political mileage from Kathikudam, only opposition from Local Committee."

The sludge trade

One issue that has caused utmost environmental concern was the disposal of the sludge. The increase in the quantity of sludge from 750 tonne to 18000 tonne a year has made disposal still more difficult. Another estimate was that the company was producing 36,000 tonnes a year or 100 tonnes a day[28]. Transportation of sludge in the semi solid form the company to outside places is prohibited by the Pollution Control Board. The maximum sludge the company could produce was only 750 tonnes a year as per the consent granted by PCB. The company's efforts at disposal of sludge in the premises of company no longer worked as popular resistance against such a measure increased. Secondly, the company no longer could hold the burgeoning amount of waste in its own premises. The NGIL has been consistently maintaining that the sludge they produce is non-toxic. The company says: "The Kerala Agricultural University and Tamil Nadu Agricultural University have conducted a study on the sludge generated by the company and certified that the ETP sludge is the co-source organic manure. The Pollution Control Board has given a certificate to the effect that ETP sludge is non hazardous in nature"[29]. The NGIL said the ETP sludge produced from its ossein unit at Kathikudam was declared completely non-hazardous by the Ministry of Environment and Forests through its order No. 23-24/2007 HSMD dt.03.01.2008. No hazardous material was being used at any stage of ossein production, said the company. The company also cited the Kerala State Pollution Control Board letter no.PCB/HO/TSR/ICO/80/2007 dt.09.02.2010 granting it permission to make compost from ETP sludge[30]. The PCB argued at the National Green Tribunal that the sledge generated at the company was not 'hazardous' as per the Hazardous Waste (Management and Transboundary Movement) rules, 2016 and therefore, authorization for handling the sledge waste is not mandatory (page 99, NGT order).

For long the company has been illegally dumping waste sludge in plantations in the guise of organic manure. This has resulted in open clash with the agents and the transport workers. An agricultural farm in Kaliyampara, Muthalamada village in Palakkad District was providing facilities for dumping the sludge waste from 2009. When it was resisted by the local people, the owner went to court and obtained police protection (WP No.29365 of 2009 dated 16 November 2009). Since then the 70 acre farm was receiving 'organic manure' in huge quantities, much in excess of a farm land ordinarily requires. The Division Bench of the Kerala High Court, while disposing a writ petition said that "due to indiscriminate dumping of the industrial waste in the property of the petitioner, the life of the people in the locality has become miserable and they are subjected to serious health hazards" (WP No.2548 g 216 (p) dated 1 August, 2016). In another incident the sludge waste dumped at Pollachi was directed to be removed within 24 hours and the NGIL had to oblige.

Production and sale of 'organic manure' in the name 'nutrisoil' was a clever tactics employed by the company to transport waste outside NGIL premises in Kathikudam. Under a non-toxicity certificate the company was trying to smuggle out the waste in the form of organic manure. Through this dirty business the company has been making huge money. The company was able to hoodwink the farmers to believe that it is a nutrition supplement to crops. "The company is shirking its responsibility and the accumulated sludge is creating horrible odor, nuisance and suffocation to the people of the locality" contented Kadukutty Panchayat who is a respondent in the Writ Petitions No.305 of 2013, No.309 of 2013 and No.149 of 2015 in the National Green Tribunal. The company has betrayed the farmers by marketing its highly hazardous sludge as compost manure of good quality, accused the Jananeethi Report. Analysis of the samples of solid waste in the Radiotracer laboratory of the Kerala Agricultural University in 2010 showed 2485 mg/kg of lead and 450 mg/kg of nickel. The maximum permissible limit of lead and nickel in organic manure in India is 100 and 50 mg/kg respectively[31] The NEERI report submitted to the NGT however, did not deal with the disposal of sludge waste.

A study for the company

As directed by the High Court of Kerala (WP (C) No.15795 of 2013, order dated 03.12.2013) the National Environmental Engineering Research Institute (NEERI), conducted a detailed study on the pollution status with respect to the Air, Water and Solid waste generated from the company. The NEERI study was held during January-February 2014 and the report was submitted in May. The report absolved the company of all its environmental wrongdoings. The NEERI says that "the concentration of the physicochemical parameters in the final treated effluent from ETP conformed to the stipulated limits of the KSPCB for discharge into Inland Surface Waters as per consent with respect to all the parameters". Most alarmingly the report adds that the heavy metals concentration in the final treated effluent from ETP was in very low concentration and of below detectable limits. It was further noted that the treated effluent samples were nontoxic to fish. Characteristics of surface water collected from Chalakkudy river from 2 km upstream of water intake well of the industry to 17.18 km downstream of treated effluent discharge location do not indicate high concentration of any major pollutants. The Ambient Air Quality in reference to the parameters namely, SO2, NO2, H2S and NH3 are within the industry premises and surrounding areas were also found within the norms prescribed by the National Ambient Air Quality Standards.

CPCB Report, a ray of hope

Based on the National Green Tribunal (NGT) direction, the Central Pollution Control Board (CPCB) made a study in October 2016. The CPCB report dated 7 November 2016 confirmed a high level of pollution caused by Nitta Gelatin company at Kathikudam.

The major suggestions made by CPCB with regard to NGIL are: To conduct third party analysis through NABL accredited Laboratory for presence of mercury in HCl before using in the process; to install separate flow meters to quantify the water consumption for domestic usage and manufacturing process; to install flow meters at ETP inlet and outlet to quantify waste water generation and its discharge to assess the actual quantification; to ensure proper scientific operation and maintenance of

ETP to meet the standards prescribed without dilution; to re-lay the existing discharge pipeline (900mts) above ground level in a time-bound manner; to ensure the continuous operation & maintenance (i.e.24 X 7) of bio filters in order to avoid odour nuisance in unit premises; to operate the continuous ambient air quality monitoring station as per norms at appropriate location which is fee from obstructions; to take necessary steps for removal and safe disposal of unutilized sludge dumped at Kaliyapuram in Palakkad at the earliest possible time. In addition, the KSPCB was directed to (1) amend the consent condition for installation of electromagnetic flow meters at ETP inlet & outlet;(2) to meet the standards for TDS and Chlorides in consent condition in tune with drinking water standards as the treated effluent is discharged into the river;(3) to instruct that no solid waste are to be stored and accumulated anywhere unscientifically in the unit, even though the ETP sludge is declared as non-hazardous.

The Action Council had demanded the closure of the factory in view of the serious findings made by the CPCB. The Action Council has demanded immediate closure of the company in the wake of the report by the Central Pollution Control Board. Council members said that the report affirmed the issues they had been raising for the past eight years. Daisy Francis, former Panchayat President of Kadukutti and member of NGIL Action Council said that the report by NPCB had rejected study reports by National Environmental Engineering Research Institute (NEERI) and Kerala State Pollution Control Board (KSPCB). The NPCB report had also listed grave lapses from the side of KSPCB, she said. V K Mohanan, another member of the Action Council said that the NPCB report had named the firm as 'habitual offender' in terms of pollution[32].

The NGT blues

Separate writs (application numbers Nos. 305, 309 of 2013 and 149 of 2015 (SZ), by Thressiamma Mathew, K.N. Lohithakshan, V.R. Babu, all from Kathikudam, were filed before the NGT. The petitioners' prayer was to ensure 'zero liquid discharge' to the Chalakudy river by NGIL and to order KPCB not to renew the Consent granted to the company if it did not comply with the siting parameters. The petitioners wanted a direction to complete the pollution control measures at the company as per the Government Order dated 03.11.2011 latest by January 2013 and to depute an expert committee to supervise the movement of ETP sludge from the company to distant places. The National Green Tribunal Order (27th February, 2017) did not address major environmental issues caused by the company. As such it did not satisfy the Action Council engaged in the fight against the company.

Some of the issues the court addressed were the following: The company should install separate flow meters to quantify the water consumption; for domestic usage and manufacturing process. The court asked the company to install flow meters at the ETP inlet and outlet to quantify the waste water generation and its discharge to assess the actual quantity. The court asked the company to achieve Zero Liquid Discharge (ZLD) to the maximum possible extends. A sewage treatment Plant was to be set up to treat the domestic sewage generated within the premises. The court wanted to operate the continuous Ambient Air Quality monitoring system as per norms. The order maintained that the existing discharge pipeline should be re-laid above the ground level which takes the treated effluent from the ETP to the Chalakkudy river. The bench directed the company to take immediate steps for the removal and safe disposal of unutilised sludge dumped at Kaliyapuram of Palakkd district within four months from the date of the judgment. The company should also take steps for the removal and safe disposal of all sludge generated and stored within the factory premises within a period of six months. The court asked the KSPCB to amend the conditions in the consent granted to the industry, by installing electro-magnetic flow meters at the ETP inlet and outlet. The KSPCB was asked to inspect the industry once in every three months and monitor the working of the industry its progress in the implementation of the directions issued and its effect on the environment and ecology. The KSPCB was to conduct periodic audit of the materials consumed and the effluents discharged by the industry. Such audit is necessary for balancing the materials including water consumption and the effluents being discharged/disposed, so as to avoid any possibility of polluting the water, environment and ecology.

Despite its bulkiness, the judgment did not categorically pin down the Nitta Gelatine company for its environmental violations. The NGT gave almost a clean chit to the Nitta Gelatin plant at Kathikudam in Thrissur came as a surprise to the activists engaged in a struggle against the plant for the past many years. According to them, the 227-page judgment is a bundle of contradictions. The judgment quoted the conclusions reached by other agencies to state that "there is no material to establish that the industry has discharged sludge along with the treated liquid effluent into the Chalakkudy river"[33] "Earlier, the KSPCB and National Environmental Engineering Research Institute (NEERI) had given clean chit to the NGIL. But an inspection conducted by National Pollution Control Board (NPCB) identified several lapses on the part of the company . It is the report submitted by the NPCB that paved way for current verdict by the NGT," said NGIL Action Council president Jaison Panikulangara[34] NGT sets 'zero discharge' deadline for Nitta Gelatin India Ltd, Times of India, February 28, 2017.

Conclusion

The NGIL agitation in many ways represented the success of a community against the might of a multinational industrial giant. Though the affected people failed to put up a collective show of force, because of political differences and internal squabbles, the perseverance of people is something amazing. The agitation brought to the fore the dilemma and contradiction in the mainstream developmental thinking so deep-rooted in the minds of people. The agitation against the factory was made out into a case between corporate greed and livelihood security of people. The agitation further revealed bias of state agencies entrusted with the task of pollution abatement.

References

Abraham C. M. (1999) Environmental Jurisprudence in India, London: Kluwer Law International.

Dwivedi G. (2011) Revisiting Important Water Conflicts in Kerala, Chalakudy, Kerala State Centre of Forum for Policy Dialogue on Water Conflicts in India And Chalakudy Puzha Samrakshana Samithi.

Iyer, V. R. Krishna (2007) Industrialise and Perish, Mainstream, Volume XLIV, No.51, 24 April.

Natraj V.K., Kamalesh Misra and Neeru Kapoor (2005) eds., Gandhian Alternative (vol. 4: Economics Where People Matter), New Delhi: Concept Publishing Company.

Seethi K. M. (2000) Cleaning Chaliyar: Pollution Control or Jobs, Economic and Political Weekly, January 15.

Notes

1. Aditi Wanchoo,Toxic Pollution, http://www.greenpeace.org/india/global/india/report/2004/11/toxics-pollution.pdf
2. V.T Padma nabahan and Joseph Makkolikkal " Ita Ita I am in pain" Mathrubhumi Weekly, November 10-16, 2013 pp.32-35.
3. Kathikudam Calling; the Last Call, Keraleeyam, June 2013, p.18.
4. Mathrubhoomi, November 10, 2013.
5. Interview with Shaju Joseph 4 January 2005
6. Interview with M T Ramesh, 21 September 2014.

7. The history of Kathikudam agitation that the Company Sought to Erase", Keraleeyam September 2013, p.33.
8. Interview with T.T. Chandrasekharan October 3, 2014.
9. Keraleeyam, September 2013.
10. Madhyamam Weekly, January 31, 2011.
11. Interview with Mirzad, District Committee Member of Solidarity, 14 September 2014.
12. The Kerala Panchayat Raj Act 1994 (Act 13 of 1994)
13. Malayala Manorama, 9 November 2011.
14. Interview with T T Chandrasekharan 3 Oct 2014.
15. G.O. (RT) No. 129/2011/Industries dated 27.01.2011.
16. G.O. (RT) No.1376/2011/1D dated 03.11.2011).
17. Malayala Manorama, 8 December 2011.
18. Keraleeyam June 2013.
19 Interview with T.R. Premkumar, 30 September 2014.
20. States Approach towards Popular Protests, Keraleeyam, July-August 2013.
21. P.G. Hari,"To T.N. Prathapan and the Protesters" Keraleeyam, July-August 2013.
22. Interview with Ayesha 21 September 2014.
23. Interview with T T Chandrasekharan, 3 October 2014
24. Interview with Suresh Kumar. 15 September 2014
25. Interview with T.R. Premkumar 22 September 2014
26. 'Kathikudam, Company Pipe in Crisis'Keralyeeam, 2013 October
27. Interview with C.D. Paul, 8 September, 2014.
28. V R Babu in WP 149/2015 before the NGT Southern Zone, Chennai.
29. NGIL counter affidavit to Writ Petitions No.305 of 2013, No.309 of 2013 and No.149 of 2015 to the National Green Tribunal, Chennai Bench.
30. Nitta Gelatine denies dumping hazardous waste, The Hindu, July 20, 2014.
31. Padmanabhan V T and Joseph Makkolil 'Contamination of the food chain by toxic metals and chemicals from a gelatin factory in Kerala, India'1. http://vixra.org/pdf/1410.0151v1.pdf.
32. Action Council for closure of Nitta Gelatin plant, Times of India, Nov 22, 2016.
33. 'Green activists need a better legal vigil', Deccan Chronicle, Apr 24, 2017, http://www.deccanchronicle.com/nation/in-other-news/240417/green-activists-need-a-better-legal-vigil.html).

Index

K

L

T